BENT

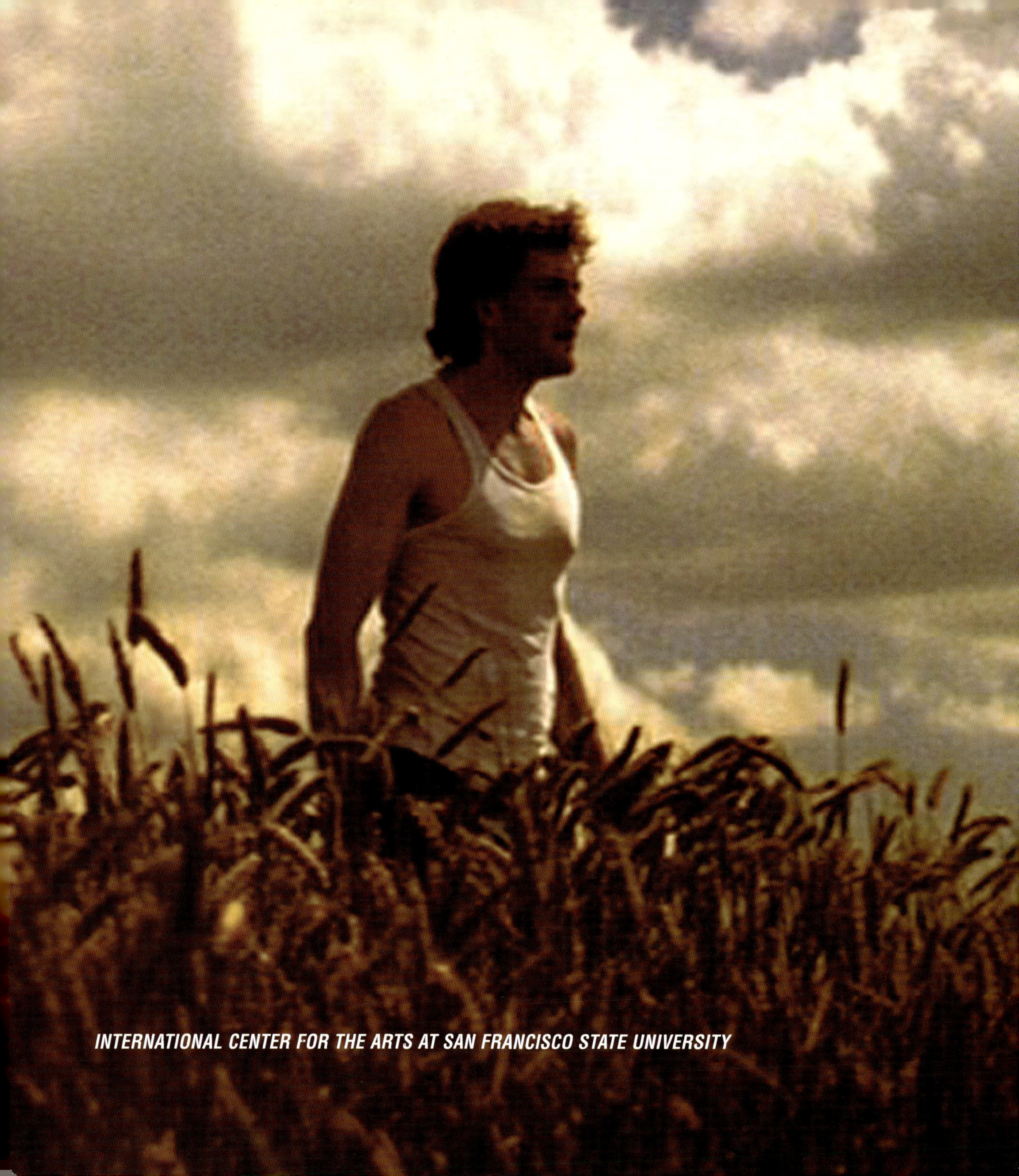
INTERNATIONAL CENTER FOR THE ARTS AT SAN FRANCISCO STATE UNIVERSITY

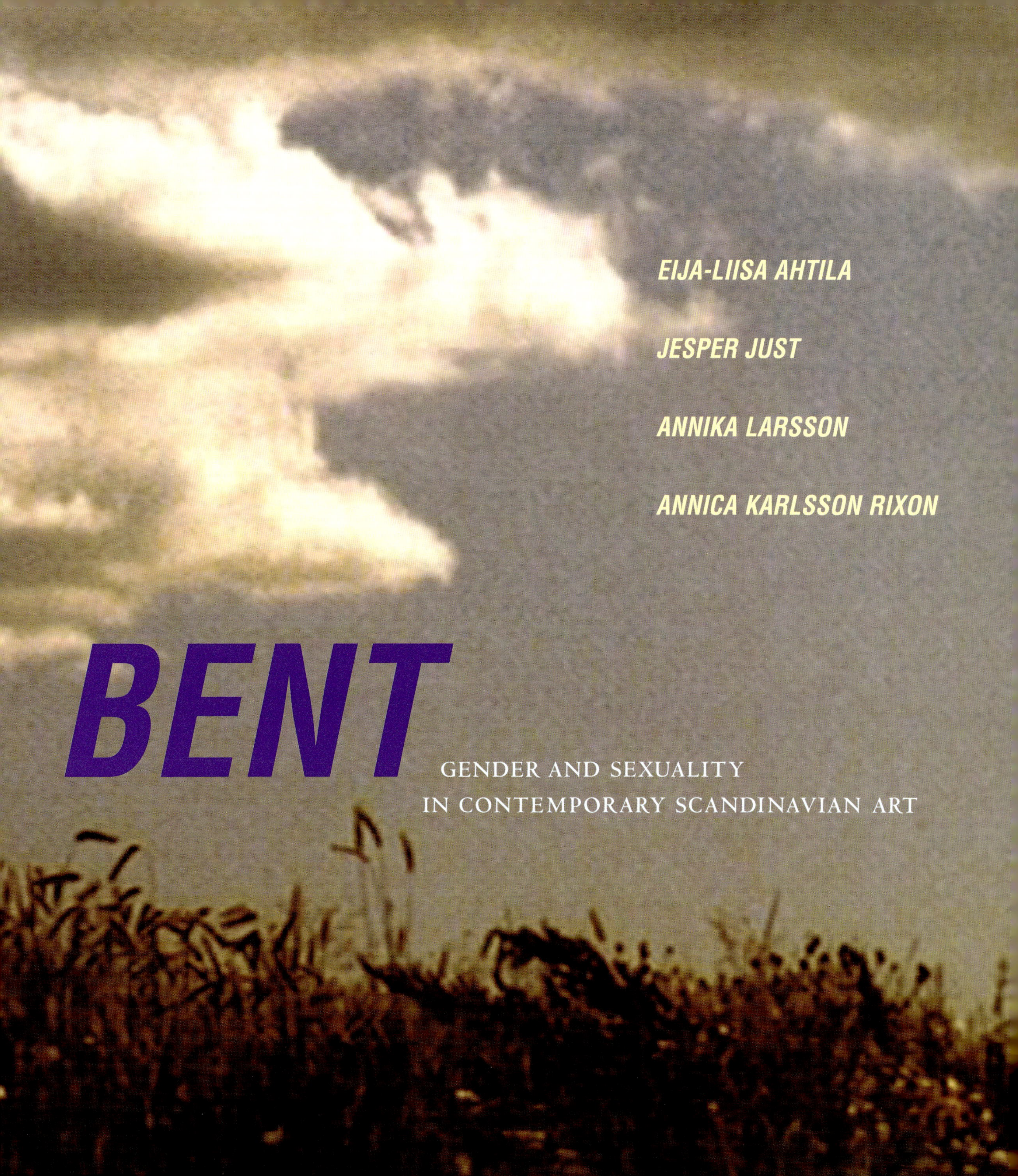
EIJA-LIISA AHTILA
JESPER JUST
ANNIKA LARSSON
ANNICA KARLSSON RIXON
BENT
GENDER AND SEXUALITY
IN CONTEMPORARY SCANDINAVIAN ART

BENT: Gender and Sexuality in Contemporary Scandinavian Art
Whitney Chadwick, editor

With contributions by:
Whitney Chadwick
Annika Öhrner
Linda Haverty Rugg

BENT: Gender and Sexuality in Contemporary Scandinavian Art is published on the occasion of an exhibition of the same title organized by the Fine Arts Gallery/International Center for the Arts, College of Creative Arts, San Francisco State University, February 2006

ISBN 0-295-98613-1
Printed in Hong Kong

© 2006 San Francisco State University
1600 Holloway Avenue
San Francisco, California 94132

Distributed by University of Washington Press
P. O. Box 50096
Seattle, WA 98145-5096
www.washington.edu/uwpress

Major support for this project provided by
The George and Judy Marcus Family

Additional support provided by
San Francisco State University
IASPIS
American Scandinavian Foundation
The Danish Arts Council
The Moderna Museet, Stockholm, Sweden
Uppsala University, Uppsala, Sweden

Fine Arts Gallery Director: Mark Dean Johnson
Fine Arts Gallery Manager & Managing Editor:
Sharon E. Bliss
Copyediting: Mark Chambers
Design: Jody Hanson
Translation: Karin Seeman

Exhibition dates:
Fine Arts Gallery, San Francisco State University, San Francisco, CA
February 11–March 16, 2006

SPECIAL THANKS
Eija-Liisa Ahtila
Jesper Just
Annika Larsson
Annica Karlsson Rixon
Crystal Eye
Marian Goodman Gallery
Perry Rubenstein Gallery
Andrea Rosen Gallery
Galleri Christina Wilson, Copenhagen
San Francisco Museum of Modern Art
Göteborg Museum of Art, Gothenburg, Sweden
The Consulate General of Sweden in San Francisco

Ariane Bicho
Mark Chambers
Wan-Lee Cheng
SFSU President and Mrs. Robert A. Corrigan
Candace Crockett
Susan Hall
Jody Hanson
Mahri Holt
Mohammad Kowsar
Tom Luddy
Alexandria Marcus
George and Judy Marcus
Mary Jane Marcus
Martin Mueller
Barbro Osher
Ulla Reilly
Andrew Speight
Stephen Ujlaki
and the students, staff, and faculty of
San Francisco State University

Frontispiece:
Jesper Just, still from *Bliss and Heaven*, 2004
Super 16mm, 7:30 minutes
Courtesy of the artist; Galleri Christina Wilson, Copenhagen; and Perry Rubenstein Gallery, New York

CONTENTS

FOREWORD

With the publication of this catalogue and the opening of the exhibit it accompanies, an idea that began to take shape almost four years ago has been expanded and vividly realized.

The first step was a campus visit by a delegation from Sweden, brought here by Barbro Osher, Consul General of Sweden in San Francisco. I and others met with the group, discussing, among other things, our mutual interest in increasing educational exchanges between two West Coast institutions that had much in common: the University of Gothenburg and San Francisco State University.

Our cities, too, are in many ways sisters. We share, among other things, a strong labor history, a passion for equal rights, and a love of the arts. We both are high-tech centers, known for innovation. All this made the possibility of partnership particularly appealing.

By happy coincidence, I have warm, personal memories of the University of Gothenburg and of Scandinavia. As a young faculty member in American Studies, I spent three years teaching at the University as a Smith-Mundt Professor and Fulbright lecturer. Those years were a revelation. I discovered that I had not truly understood my own culture until I stood outside of it. That experience convinced me that internationalizing U.S. higher education was—and is—a critical mission.

Another convergence advanced this project. We are fortunate to have on our faculty the noted art historian Whitney Chadwick, who has a close relationship with the University of Gothenburg. *BENT* began to take shape. The show, with its focus on gender and illustration of how differently it can be viewed by another culture, is particularly appropriate for a university that is nationally recognized as a leader in human sexuality studies and research.

Thanks to a timely and generous gift, we have been able to place *BENT* in a larger artistic context. With the inauguration in 2004 of the International Center for the Arts (ICA) at San Francisco State University, we, and all arts lovers, gained a thrilling new resource. Made possible by the generosity of San Francisco State University alumni George and Judy Marcus, the ICA was established to celebrate some of the world's most innovative art and artists, cultivating and presenting a broad vision of global arts and culture.

With the opening of *BENT: Gender and Sexuality in Contemporary Scandinavian Art,* the ICA marks the start of "Bridging the Baltic," an entire spring season of programming celebrating a region of the world that has made major contributions to the arts.

All this is a magnificent outcome, and it could not have been realized without the work and help of many friends—at the University, in the community, in Sweden, and throughout the Baltic. To all of them, I extend our warm thanks and appreciation.

— Robert A. Corrigan, president
San Francisco State University

THE MEDIUM IS NOT THE MESSAGE

Whitney Chadwick

STOCKHOLM, JULY 2005. *Images of the summer's Live 8 concerts flash across the television screen—London, Johannesburg, Tokyo, African children, Madonna; a worldwide kaleidoscope of satellite-dispersed images. With one eye on the television, the other on the catalogue of* Implosion: A Post-Modern Perspective *(1987), the first major museum exhibition in Sweden to focus on the "information age" and its worldwide dissemination of mass-media images, I am struck by curator Lars Nittve's prescient commentary on that year's Live Aid concerts, the antecedent to today's events: "the first global entertainment event . . . beamed from continent to continent. . . . It was obvious that this was real Live Aid music: an original multiethnic synthesis without any 'originals,' a product that transformed the event's explosion across borders into an all-consuming implosion."* [1]

The *Implosion* exhibition brought together the work of several generations of conceptually based and/or "project-oriented" contemporary artists at a moment when concepts of history and nature; the authentic and the simulated; and gender, sexual, and cultural identities were the subject of widespread discussion. Appropriation, documentation, and gender and social analysis in media-based genres—film, photography, video, advertising—were already evident in the work of younger Scandinavian artists. They also drew from Nordic traditions of documentary work in photography, film, text, and installation, from histories of progressive social policies committed to gender equality, environmental sustainability, and social responsibility, and from the examples of prominent artists of the 1960s and 1970s such as Christer Strömholm, Oyvind Fahlström, and others.

Expansion of the European Union (Denmark, Finland, and Sweden became members by slim majorities) drew international attention to Sweden's progressive social policies in areas of gender equality and parental leave. European Union membership also encouraged Nordic countries to expand government-sponsored programs supporting artists and international exhibitions.[2] During the 1980s, a revival in the film industry saw the work of Aki and Mika Kaurismäki and Lars von Trier become as internationally known as that of Ingmar Bergman. In music, performers from Björk to Aqua shot to the top of the pop charts, while in the visual arts, artists increasingly lived and worked transnationally.

Eija-Liisa Ahtila, Jesper Just, Annika Larsson, and Annica Karlsson Rixon are four Nordic artists whose work emerged between 1987 (Ahtila) and 1999 (Just). Like many of their contemporaries, all have studied, lived, and worked abroad, and their work shares an acceptance of the conventions of photographic/cinematic media and engages in processes of art historical and/or cultural appropriation that challenge the viewer to reexperience and rethink the relationship between individual perceptions and social meaning, and between the mediated image and the visible world. Theoretically sophisticated, though not primarily "about" theory, their artistic practices embrace the imagery of art history and popular culture while retaining a critical, sometimes ironic relationship to its sources.

Still one might ask why we have chosen to bring these particular artists together in an exhibition in California. And why we have linked their work to *gender* and *sexuality*, words often colored by their association with the sexual and cultural politics of the 1970s and 1980s.[3] Although we do so as part of a university-wide arts festival that in 2006 will focus on the Baltic region, it is not with the intention of seeking out a shared or "authentic" Nordic or Scandinavian sensibility in their work. Nor do we wish to define their work in terms of a politics. Instead we are interested in looking at the diverse ways their individual artistic practices map new relationships between individual expression and social context, and the ways that these strategies may illuminate formations of social, sexual, and personal identity within visual representation.[4] Although the individual practices of all four artists have been shaped by their engagement with the conventions of pictorial, cinematic, and photographic representation, their specific responses to their sources diverge.

Ahtila and Karlsson Rixon, both art students in the 1980s (Ahtila at Helsinki University, Karlsson Rixon at the Nordic School of Photography in Sweden), were educated during a period when influential feminist critical and theoretical texts, including Laura Mulvey's *Visual Pleasure and Narrative Cinema* (1975) and Griselda Pollock's

Vision, Voice and Power: Feminist Art History and Marxism (1982), circulated internationally in the pages of *Screen, Block, m/f,* and other British publications. The visibility of Pollock and other feminist scholars as lecturers, and the presence of a strong historical feminist tradition in Scandinavia, contributed to a growing interest in feminist critiques of patriarchy.

Ahtila's first public exhibitions and collaborative performances, *A Short Cultural-Political Quadrille* and *The Nature of Things* (both developed with Maria Ruotsala), took place around the same time as *Implosion*. *Quadrille,* featured in the 1987 Lahti AV Biennial, was organized around a polemical dialogue on the building of a new arts museum. The performance combined manipulated and altered images of ancient Greek and Roman sculptures, modern European architecture, vignettes in which the two women imitated classical Greek sculptures, and verbal texts in which they discussed the future of the art museum at the end of the twentieth century. Although informed by feminist critiques, the performance engaged a wider politics of representation that supported a critique of the museum as a repository of eternal cultural "truth." In an earlier video, *The Nature of Things,* the two artists enumerated the imaginary attributes of familiar consumer objects ("original," "revealing," "sensual") and reclined in poses derived from the visual conventions of television commercials. They concluded with a deadpan recitation of familiar brand names, from Nokia to MasterCard, in an ironic parody of consumer culture's tendency to fetishize commodities and define identity through material possessions.[5] *Quadrille* and *The Nature of Things* marked the beginning of a series of increasingly complex video and film installations in which Ahtila would explore the ways that the representations of mass culture, social convention, and personal relationships structure subjectivity and identity.

The early work of Ahtila and Karlsson Rixon frames questions of personal identity within matrices of human relations, work, everyday life, and social and historical constructions of identity. Focusing on still photography rather than the moving image, Karlsson Rixon shifted between a socially involved documentary tradition in Swedish photography—exemplified in the work of influential photographers and teachers such as Christer Strömholm—and a desire to use the camera as a tool for investigating and shaping personal reality and social identity, an interest she shared with artists such as Annika von Hausswolff, Annika Eriksson, Miriam Bäckström, and others.[6]

While living in Los Angeles and attending the California Institute of the Arts in the early 1990s, Karlsson Rixon began to investigate the historical relationship between painting and photography. Already familiar with the community of Nordic painters active in the village of Skagen on Denmark's north coast at the end of the nineteenth and beginning of the twentieth centuries, she was drawn to their Nordic version of the Impressionists' search to capture the modern world in scenes of everyday life revealed through the transitory effects of light and atmosphere. A stranger in a southern California landscape that was both unsettling in its unfamiliarity and strangely reassuring in its evocation of Skagen's expansive meeting of sea and sky, Karlsson Rixon began to conduct research on the work of artists such as P. S. and Marie Krøyer, Anna and Michael Ancher, and Richard Bergh. Mystified by the visual disjunction between the two figures in a double portrait of the Krøyers painted in 1890, she turned to art historian Kirk Varnedoe's recently published *Northern Light: Nordic Art at the Turn of the Century* and discovered that the explanation for the painting's conflicted representation lay, not in Krøyer's use of the camera as a source, but in the fact that the work was jointly authored (Marie had supplied her own self-portrait, a fact generally omitted from earlier literature).[7] Although a member of the first generation of professional women artists in Scandinavia, Marie Krøyer remained unable to reconcile life as an artist and life as the wife of one of Denmark's most famous painters, and the visual and social instability that Karlsson Rixon observed—accompanied by a gender bias that had effectively buried one-half of the artistic partnership—motivated her to begin an aesthetic and historical documentation of her own artistic community.

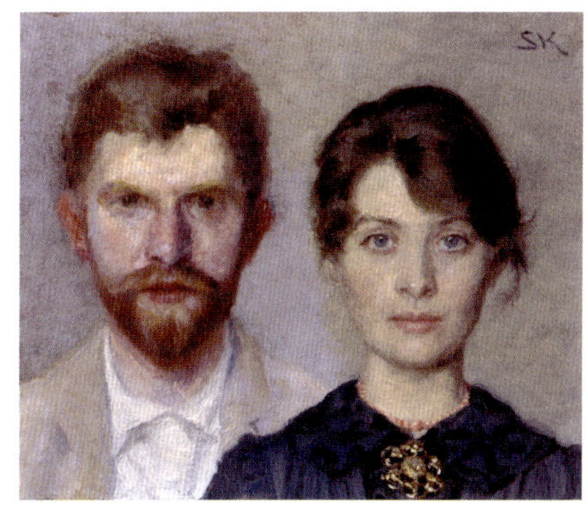

Marie and P. S. Krøyer, *Double Portrait of Marie and P. S. Krøyer*, 1890
Oil on canvas
5.9 x 7.3 in. (15 x 18.7 cm)
Collection of Skagens Museum, Denmark
Photo: Esben Thorning

In *Nordic Light* (1997–98), a series of Cibachrome photographs from California, many of them modeled after specific historical paintings from the Skagen community, Karlsson Rixon turns a keen eye on issues of personal and professional identity, friendships and relationships, the built and the natural landscapes. Her attention to interactions between humans and the natural world as they walk on the beach, meet for lunch, or relax in conversation, and her keen eye for effects of light and atmosphere, bind these images to their historical precedents, even as they remain thoroughly contemporary. The careful articulation of gender and sexual difference and the commitment to communities based on friendship and professional life also becomes an implicit response to the supercharged American art world of the 1990s with its celebration of the individual (generally male) artist as media star and celebrity. Beyond her interest in fostering a dialogue between historical painting and contemporary photography lies Karlsson Rixon's awareness of the fragility and contingency of community in an age of transnational dislocation, her recognition of the role of the photograph as a marker of lived experience, and her growing realization that the photograph might function to produce, as well as record, the real.

The photograph *Early Summer Evening in Los Angeles* (1997) references an earlier summer evening captured in Bergh's well-known *Nordic Summer Evening* (1899–1900).

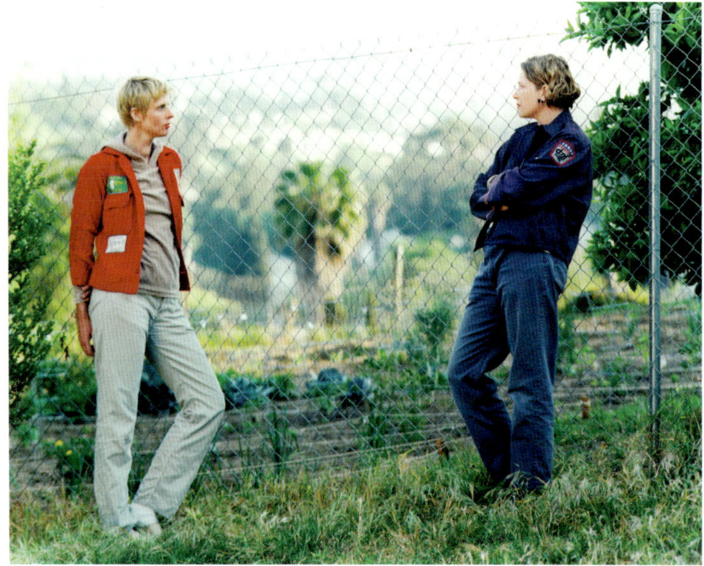

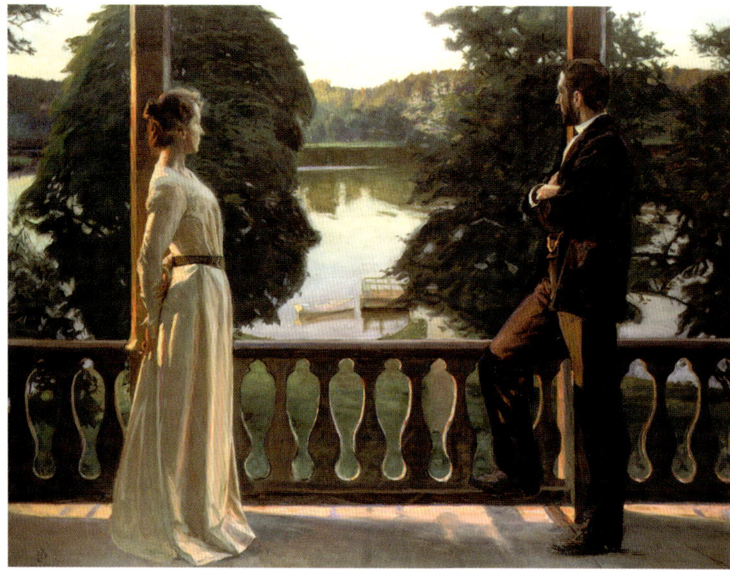

Annica Karlsson Rixon, *Early Summer Evening in Los Angeles* from the series *Portraits in Nordic Light*, 1997
C print
46.8 x 62.4 in. (120 x 160 cm)
Courtesy of the artist

Richard Bergh, *Nordic Summer Evening*, 1899–1900
Oil on canvas
66.3 x 87 in. (170 x 223 cm)
Collection of Göteborg Museum of Art
Photo: Ebbe Carlsson

A middle-class couple stand at opposite ends of a long balcony contemplating an evening landscape of idyllic peacefulness. The two figures, physically separate but spiritually united in their contemplation of nature, reinforce a modernist social ideology that sought to reconcile social and cultural change within a commitment to the pleasures of everyday life lived in harmony with the natural world. Karlsson Rixon's contemplative figures are equally still, self-contained, and historically specific in costume and attitude. Yet, the two women's gazes neither meet nor contemplate the landscape between them, and they inhabit a social world in which models of bourgeois heterosexuality can no longer be assumed. Instead there is a play of sameness and difference, desire and avoidance. Bergh's pristine nature has given way to a late-twentieth-century urban sprawl. A chain-link fence separates the two women from a garden in which vegetables grow in tight rows in the foreground and identical suburban houses threaten to consume a hillside in the distance.

The shifting boundaries between fictive and "real" space, the contingent nature of subjectivity as it is formed through cultural mediations, and the impossibility of "knowing" with certitude also form the core of Eija-Liisa Ahtila's investigations into human relationships, sexuality, and death during the 1990s. Her appropriation and subversion of the conventions of cinematic and televisual forms merged documentary objectivity, everyday detail, and fiction in installations that often combine projections and dispersed sound. The works in the mini-film trilogy *Me/We, Okay,* and *Gray* (1993), shot in black-and-white and projected on three monitors, is the first of Ahtila's works shot for television, and the first to deliberately break the distinction between fiction and advertising and initiate the multiplicity of speaking positions that would be more fully developed in subsequent works.[8] Shifting between vivid evocations of specific incidents and a verbal polyphony that resists narrative wholeness, the work recalls both the literary narrative structures of the novels of William Faulkner and James Joyce and psychoanalysis's linking of utterances formed around desire, loss, and repression to formations of identity. If Ahtila's works deny the viewer the fixed "gaze" that critic Laura Mulvey theorized as necessary to the maintenance of cultural binaries (male/female, self/other, etc.), they share their deconstructive strategies and investigations into formations of identity with experimental films of the 1980s, from Sally Potter's *Thriller* to Trinh T. Minh-ha's *Reassemblage*.

Ahtila also shares an introspective tradition among earlier Nordic artists from Edvard Munch and August Strindberg to Ingmar Bergman, one that often centers around evocations of the fragility and discontinuity of psychological awareness and themes of subjectivity, sexuality, and death. She has acknowledged Bergman's influence, along with that of Antonioni, Fassbinder, and the Kaurismäki brothers (whose very personal films also shift between filmic and televisual conventions).[9] Without belaboring the comparison, it is useful to consider Bergman's unraveling of traditional conceptions of gendered subjectivity and their penetrating scrutiny of female awareness, and his dismantling of the fixed oppositions between spectator and spectacle, self and other, with Ahtila's emphasis on complexity and difference, and the breakdown of the real and the imaginary in works such as *Anne, Aki, and God* (1998) and *The House* (2002). The former, a portrayal of a schizophrenic young man in search of love and the voice of God, moves skillfully through a wide range of speaking positions in what critic Daniel Birnbaum has called "an intricate mix of insane imagination and documentary footage."[10]

Bergman's notes for the film *Persona* (1966) include a description of an encounter between the actress Elisabet Vogler, who has retreated into a silence in a hospital and lies in a state between sleep and death, and her nurse Alma, in which the two women's identities appear to merge:

> She returns to the dead woman, glances shyly at her, and suddenly they *exchange personalities* [Bergman's italics]. The way, exactly how I don't know, she experiences, with a fragmentary sharpness, the condition of the other woman's soul, to the point of absurdity. She meets Mrs. Vogler, who is now Alma and speaks with her voice.[11]

The porousness of the boundaries Bergman articulates in *Persona* finds an echo in the monologue of Ahtila's protagonist, a woman named Elisa, in *The House:*

> I meet people. One at a time they come inside me and live inside me, some of them only for a moment, some stay. They set up wherever they want to and take my facial expressions or my leg's resting position and put their own in their place. They lie on my back and press their toes into my Achilles tendon. . . .[12]

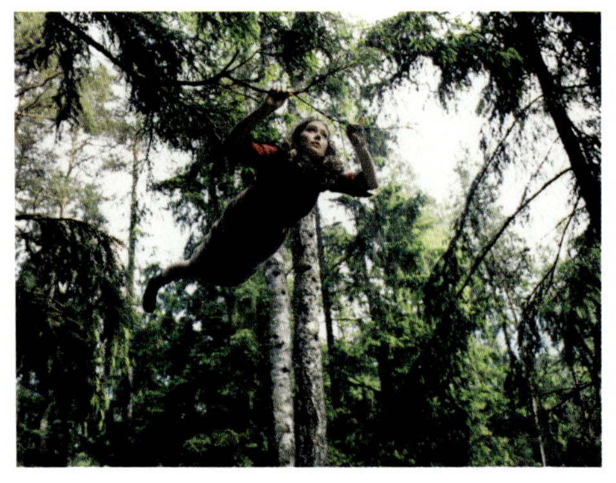

Eija-Liisa Ahtila, still from *The House*, 2002
DVD multiscreen installation, 14:00 minutes
Courtesy of Marian Goodman Gallery, New York

In *The House* and other related works, including *Lahja* (The Present; 2001) and *The Wind* (2002), the introduction of multiple voices speaking through one mouth, or the same voice through many mouths, often underscores the speaking subject's emotional and/or psychological instability, a psychic space reinforced by the use of multiple screens. *Lahja* is a five-monitor installation showing five short independent stories. Running on a loop, and varying from one to two minutes, the stories play simultaneously. Another series of 30-second TV spots made at the same time as the filmed stories is intended to be shown on television as advertising spots throughout the exhibition. If the work's subject is the fictionalized stories and personal worlds of women who have developed psychoses, its theme is forgiveness, expressed in a text—"Give yourself a present, forgive yourself"—shown at the end of each story and incorporated into the gallery installation in the form of blankets embroidered with the same message, which are for sale. The multiplicity of forms of address and multiple viewing contexts underscore Ahtila's interest in reaching out to different contexts and audiences.

Ahtila's work was included in *Nuit blånche: scènes nordiques: les années 90* (1998), a large survey of Nordic art of the 1980s and 1990s organized by the Musée d'Art Moderne de la Ville de Paris. The exhibition, which linked an earlier expressionist tradition in Nordic art to the recent emergence of international neo-expressionism in European and North American painting and sculpture, marked a shift in the reception of contemporary Nordic art outside Scandinavia. If *Implosion* had imported international postmodernism into Sweden, *Nuit blånche* signaled southern Europe's embrace of a new regional cultural dynamism in the arts. The so-called Nordic miracle became a way to characterize the emergence of a northern decentralized regional cultural network that operated both locally and globally, even as the growing challenges of immigration, cultural diversity, integration, and shrinking resources in what had previously been relatively homogeneous cultures ensured that new directions in the arts would not assume idealist or utopian dimensions.[13]

By the end of the 1990s, the Nordic countries and their artists had assumed high visibility in what many now refer to as a "transnational" art world, one tied to geographic dislocation, postcolonial renegotiations of the relationship between centers and margins, and globalizing tendencies. Much art of the 1990s and the first decade of the twenty-first century would remain closely linked to the genres of photography/video/film and installation.

Annika Larsson and Jesper Just's work dates from the late 1990s and early 2000s. Both employ video and film in narratives that fuse fictionalized "plots" and images appropriated from Hollywood film, popular music, and the Internet. Larsson began clipping and archiving magazine pictures and filming directly from the TV screen while still a student at Royal College of Fine Art in Stockholm. Excited by the fine line between control and catastrophe in a 1997 performance in which she had herself driven to the edge of a Gotland stone quarry each day, but frustrated by her inability to "see" the work while inside it, she turned to video as a medium.

A series of works from 1998 and 1999, including *Herr B, Cigar, Tanning Man,* and *Covered Car,* introduce masculinity and its visual codes as her primary subject. Like Just, she focuses on a particular kind of masculinity, one embodied in the actions and interactions of ordinary-looking white men, often in suits. Like Richard Prince's appropriated photographs of male models in the 1970s, Larsson's first video pieces expose masculinity as a carefully constructed "look." Uninterested in critiques of male power, Larsson viewed her models as readymades, and she adopted a Duchampian stance toward them as a "product already created and ready to be used."[14] It is the abstractness of the look of middle-class corporate masculinity, its mild ordinariness, and what she sees as a suggestion of vulnerability conveyed through the reliance on a "uniform" that attracted her.[15] Although she uses actors, she relies heavily on details of men's suits downloaded from online store "dummies," appropriating advertising's fragmented images and combining them with close-ups of mouths smoking and signifiers of masculinity (competitive games, cigars, luxury cars, and so on). Throughout, Larsson's approach remains locked to directing the gaze and asserting visual control.

Larsson's most provocative foray into ritualized behavior remains *Dog* (2001), in which two men in suits, one shown with a whistle in his mouth holding the leash of a large collared dog, engage in a series of ambiguous slow-motion actions. The almost balletic gestures and movements between the figures, the choreographed touching and stroking of the dog, along with lingering focus on details, suggest fetishized looking, or rituals of dominance and submission. But Larsson is careful to withhold the contextual information that might enable more fixed readings of the imagery, and its

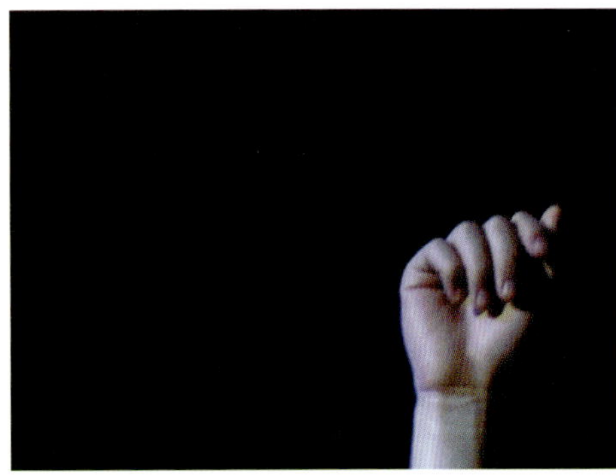

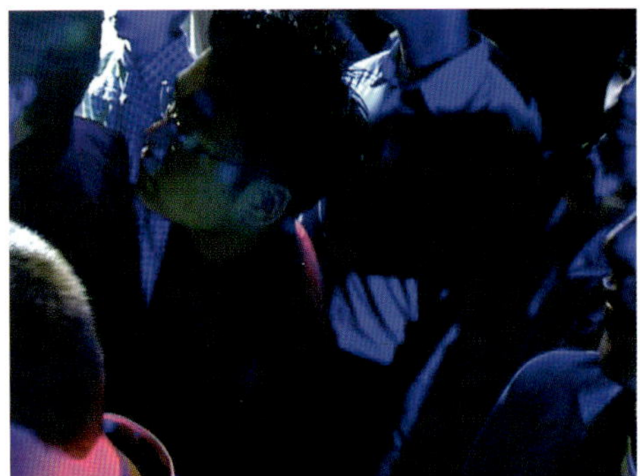

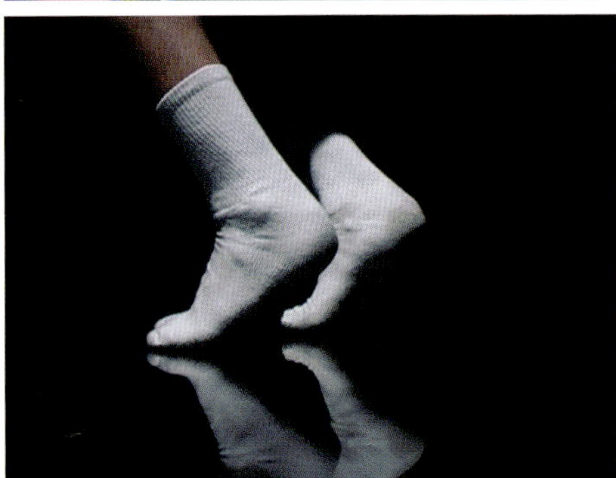

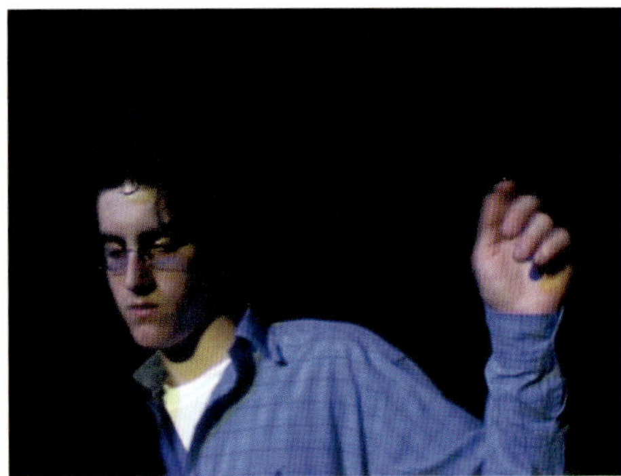

Annika Larsson, stills from *New Gravity*, 2003
DVD loop, 29:30 minutes
Courtesy of the artist and Andrea Rosen Gallery, New York

narrative openness, ambiguity, and deferrals of meaning challenge interpretation.[16] Larsson filmed while living in Berlin, where she studied historical propaganda films produced by Russian communists such as Sergei Eisenstein and Alexander Dovzhenko and German Nazi propaganda films, especially those of Leni Riefenstahl. Indeed the filming of the two figures from below against a monochrome sky and the repetitions and abstract visual details, when combined with the heroic sound track (provided by Johann Strauss's *Egyptian March* and the electronic music of Tobias Bernstrup), also encodes Riefenstahl's use of the camera to outline sculptural bodies against the sky in the diving sequence from *Olympia,* her 1936 celebration of Hitler's staging of the Olympic games in Berlin. Eschewing dialogue and voice-over, Larsson relies instead on dramatic camera angles, extreme close-ups, dramatic sound, and slow, often repeated gestures to evoke mood.

If *Dog* comes closest to fulfilling Larsson's desire to create a narrative drama that conveys a subtle erotic tension without articulation, the recent video *New Gravity* (2003) seems to represent a darker vision of contemporary culture.[17] The work's underlying theme—adolescent masculine sexual identity—is communicated by a group of teenage boys at a dance club as they interact with two figures: one a sexually ambiguous singer (played by musician and performance artist Tobias Bernstrup), the other a digitally produced animation of a "super male" figure who appears at the end of the piece. Like Eija-Liisa Ahtila's *If 6 Was 9* (1996), a video installation using three large abutted screens in which a group of teenage girls in Helsinki discuss sexuality, the subject is adolescent sexuality in relation to the imagery of popular culture—from porn magazines (Ahtila) to pop music (Larsson). Like Ahtila, Larsson also focuses on the interaction between psychic and social reality, but she does so without recourse to dialogue, relying instead on the visual expression of coded images. Like Ahtila, Larsson also maintains implications of a temporal cinematic narrative (both artists have been influenced by German film, particularly the works of Fassbinder and Wim Wenders), but Larsson's composition remains less elliptical and layered than Ahtila's work, less concerned with the relationship between interior and exterior worlds and more focused on surface and appearance. Larsson's skillful use of the visual detail is underscored in *New Gravity* by the way the visual field is broken apart by the effects of the disco's pulsing light, with its ability to fast-freeze the most minute actions, and the repetitive rhythms of the throbbing amplified music provided by Bernstrup.

Instead of dialogue, Larsson offers the boys' adolescent, perhaps atavistic response to the overstimulation of pop music playing out in the incubatory space of the dance club. As in her earlier works, Larsson takes an almost anthropological stance, substituting the computer for the tape recorder and conducting Internet "field work" in hours of online searches for particular visual "looks," which she then incorporates into her moving images.[18] In *New Gravity* the dance club, a common site of social interactions and dating rituals, becomes a psychic space in which the viewpoint shifts between the banal and the frightening. As the camera focuses on a succession of details—shoes, eyeglasses, faces—the boys' social awkwardness becomes increasingly apparent. Although the music's tempo and the physical responses it produces (combined with the stroboscopic visual effects) effectively deny the spectator the distance necessary for contemplative or analytic viewing, it is clear that the boys are not "of age," and there is a psychological disconnection between the awkward childishness of their physical movements and the sophistication of the singer whose appearance elicits their uncomfortable glances.

The opening up of this ambiguous psychic space introduces a powerful note of psychological instability. The appearance of the animated male figure, who begins interacting with one of the boys and directing his movements, introduces a shift from the "real" space of the dance club to Baudrillard's "hyperreal," a world in which images derive not from objects in the world, but only from other images. The seductions of such a world have been widely chronicled—the obsessions and addictive behaviors associated with cyberporn, computer games such as Dungeons and Dragons, and so on—and it is the blurring of the line between the real and the cyberreal that produces the video's disturbing ambiguity and makes it impossible for the viewer to assign coherent meaning to the work's final image of a boy's suspended and dangling feet. Fantasy? Suicide? Play? We will never know, for in Larsson's hands the game, the entertainment, becomes the only reality available to us. Her tight focus on the look of the familiar, elicited through constant attention to the surfaces of objects, remains a constant reminder that our vision of reality is in fact carefully crafted into surrogates, desirable commodities that take on human attributes through sophisticated manipulation. Her photographic eye for detail exposes social reality as a system of rules, a visual language divorced from individual emotion and expression, yet one that conveys the possibility of seeing the world in new ways.

Reexamining conventions that structure the way we perceive and understand the relationship between images, the social world, and the individual, Ahtila, Larsson, and Just's moving images utilize complex filmic structures to convey the intricacy of our experience of the world. Just's films—while also utilizing motifs, images, and themes appropriated from cinematic, literary, and popular music sources—also mine those sources for their ability to evoke strong human feelings. For the most part shot as films and then transferred to video, the short pieces develop from an interest in cinematography that emerged during his years as a student (Just graduated from Copenhagen's Royal Danish Academy of Fine Arts in 2003). Using words, gestures, dancing, and music, his protagonists (Just has worked extensively with the actor Johannes Lilleøre and the same crew since leaving school) act out narratives originally inspired by a particular location, the physical ambience of which suggests both the subject and the ways the space will be used cinematically. In them men—lovers or companions or fathers and sons—experiment with issues of identity as Just interweaves cinematic and musical clichés, appropriated images, the rejecting of restrictive bonds, and the performing of new social roles.[19]

Just's works center around themes of identity and human relationships between men. In *No Man Is an Island II* (2004), well-dressed white men sit alone in what appears to be the bar of a men's club, or perhaps a strip club. The room is furnished with dark leather, mirrors, large paintings of academic nudes devoid of emotional affect, and a long polished bar. Like Larsson, Just has chosen to focus his works around a particular construction of masculinity—Nordic, middle-class, professional, neatly dressed—but there the similarity between the two artists' approaches ends, for Just, unlike Larsson, teases out the emotions associated with intergenerational relationships between men.

Working with visual clichés (he often uses the raking light and deep shadow associated with noir film), Just transforms the chance encounters often associated with homoerotic desire, never explicitly articulated in his films, into occasions for the release of powerful feelings. As the ingenuous young actor enters the shadowed interior space of male fantasy—his face is caught between images of an illuminated sign marked *Toilet* and a painting of languid female nudes—and begins to sing Roy Orbison's "Crying," the bar's male patrons burst spontaneously into an a capella rendering of the song ("I'd been crying over you . . ."). Just's use of choreographed singing in his films recalls Dennis Potter's (*Pennies from Heaven*) and Lars von Trier's (*Dancer in the Dark*) reworking of similar material, but Just's incorporation of song is restricted neither to von Trier's play with the musical's conventions or Potter's use of the device as a temporary escape from his work's underlying darkness. Instead music becomes the structural vehicle through which Just's characters transcend social inhibitions and give expression to their emotions. Light from the bottles behind the bar reflects in the tears that flow from the eyes of the weeping young man as the older men's faces turn toward him in sadness and longing. For a moment, however brief, Just reclaims the emotional magic of popular film and music.

In the end, Just's appropriations of the conventions of Hollywood cinema reveal the power of mass culture's banal expressions to affect our emotions. Even so, we

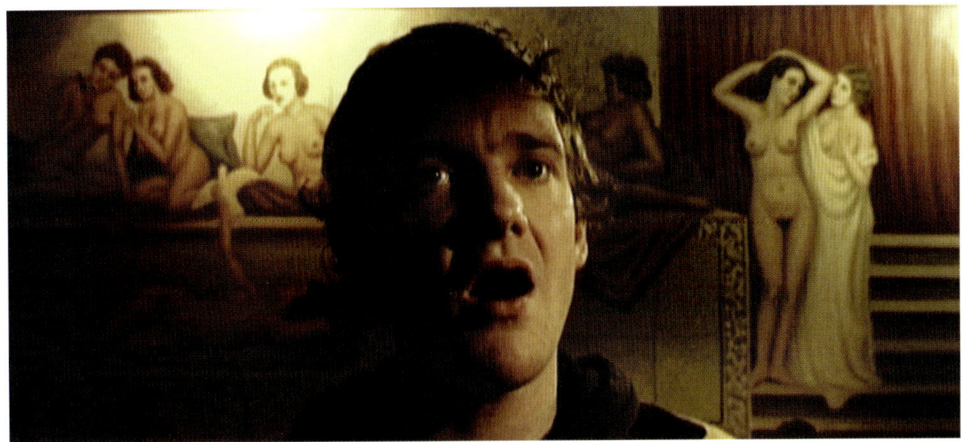

Jesper Just, still from *No Man Is an Island II,* 2004
DVCAM, 4:00 minutes
Courtesy of the artist; Galleri Christina Wilson, Copenhagen; and Perry Rubenstein Gallery, New York

remain aware of the tension between the hypermasculinity of Hollywood film and the gaze of homoerotic desire liberated by queer theory. The motif of the weeping man is repeated in *Something to Love* (2005), as we watch a car slowly enter an underground parking garage and see a close-up of the middle-aged driver's distraught face wet with tears. A young man stares, expressionless, from the back seat as the driver, still weeping, gets out, holds the door open, and watches as he disappears into an elevator before setting out in pursuit. At the top of the stairs, he confronts the young man and a blond woman locked in a passionate embrace. As he stares, their image begins to rotate like the figures on a music box and we become aware of a tinkling piano score, hairstyles that recall the 1930s, movements that replicate the startled awkwardness of a Hitchcock moment. But if the stereotypes are pure Hollywood, they are there to be shattered into new relationships—as the couple break apart, the two men return together to the parked car and drive away.

Refusing modernism's opposition to popular culture and embracing cinematic conventions that focus on the moving image's ability to invent and sustain new fictional narratives, Just engages erotic tension as ambiguous and multivalent. Although he has referred to the intergenerational male-to-male relationships in his films as alluding to—though never fully articulating—the complexities and longings of father/son bonds, the relationship between paternal love, filial devotion, and erotic tension remains elusive. In *Bliss and Heaven* (2004), Just also challenges the polarities of masculinity and femininity, reforming them into a fluid dynamic of shifting positions. While the film's title derives from a line in Stanley Kubrick's *A Clockwork Orange,* the theme is an homage to the *Beaver Trilogy,* a cult classic produced by cinematographer Trent Harris that consists of three short interlocking pieces in which a stalker pursues Olivia Newton-

John. In Just's film, we watch a young man stride across a waist-high field of grain following a long-haul truck driver. Following the object of his desire into the back of a truck, the young man finds himself the sole occupant of an otherwise empty opera house. When his quarry reappears, he wears a long blond wig and, draped in a flowing white silk scarf, sings a sentimental ballad by Olivia Newton-John ("Please Don't Keep Me Waiting") with dramatic gestures and a melancholy intensity. As critic Michael Wilson observed:

> In its theatrical delivery and ecstatic reception the performance recalls not only Dean Stockwell's lip sync to Roy Orbison's "In Dreams" in David Lynch's *Blue Velvet,* but also Mia Kushner's nightclub striptease to "Everybody Knows" by Leonard Cohen in Atom Egoyan's *Exotica.* In recognizing that Hollywood film and popular song have the power to transcend critical derision through their direct emotional appeal, Just has a direct route to the mysterious heart of relationships between men.[20]

The artists in *Bent* have all addressed the problem of the photographically derived image at a cultural moment when digitization and mass circulation have stripped the photographic (or filmic) image of any connection to literal reality. And they have done so by keeping issues of sexual, gender, and social identity alive within a forest of proliferating signs that threaten to substitute opinion for reasoned argument and reduce meaning to institutional sloganeering. While their work draws on a wide range of sources and strategies, it remains centered in the distinctive personal visions of the individual artists and in their commitment to seeing beyond conventionalized usages and readings of visual imagery.

NOTES

1. *Implosion: A Postmodern Perspective* (Stockholm: Moderna Museet, 1987), 18. Exhibition catalogue.
2. The Swedish "gender equality model" has been at the leading edge of European equal rights legislation involving public child care, dual bread-winning families, and equal rights to parental leave benefits; for more on these policies, see *Genus: A Journal from the Swedish Secretariat for Gender Research*, no. 1 (2001).
3. The term *gender* is used here to refer to social constructions of masculinity and femininity as distinct from the biologically determined categories of male and female. *Sexuality* alerts us to forms of sexual orientation and identity. Both terms take into account the ways our self-understanding is formed within the images culture provides as expressions of ideal femininity/masculinity/sexuality.
4. A number of recent exhibitions and publications in Europe have addressed these issues. For example, Kim Levin, "Nothing Left to Lose," in *Organizing Freedom: Nordic Art of the 90s*, (Stockholm: Moderna Museet, 2000), exhibition catalogue, takes a look at contemporary Nordic art from a North American feminist perspective; Daniel Birnbaum and John Peter Nilsson, eds., *Like Virginity Once Lost: Five Views on Nordic Art Now* (Stockholm: Propexus, 1999) and *Norden*, (Vienna Kunsthalle, 2000), exhibition catalogue, bring together critical perspectives from Scandinavia.
5. Ahtila's early work is discussed in Kari Yli-Annala, "Puhuvat minät/Talking Selves," *Eija-Liisa Ahtila: Fantasized Persons and Taped Conversation* (Kiasma: Kiasma Museum of Contemporary Art and London: Tate Modern, 2002), 215–219. Exhibition catalogue.
6. Critic Sara Arrhenius has written widely on the role of the documentary tradition in contemporary Nordic art, stressing the ways the genre offers an imprint or proof of a tangible real; see "Body Contact: Hungering for the Real," in Birnbaum and Nilsson, eds., *Like Virginity Once Lost*, 11–35. For a historical context, see Lena Johannesson and Gunilla Knape, eds., *Women Photographers: European Experience* (Gothenburg: Acata Universitatis Gothenburgensis, 2003). Karlsson Rixon's early work is discussed in Anna Tellgren, "Fotografi och kön: Om den fotobaserade konsten under 1990-talet," in *Från modernism till samtidskonst Svenska kvinnliga konstnärer*, eds. Yvonne Eriksson and Anette Göthlund (Lund: Bokförlaget Signum, 2003), 108–128.
7. Kirk Varnedoe, *Northern Light: Nordic Art at the Turn of the Century* (New Haven and London: Yale University Press, 1988). The book originated in the publication prepared for the exhibition *Northern Light: Realism and Symbolism in Scandinavian Painting, 1880–1910*, organized by the Brooklyn Museum of Art in 1982.
8. Terry R. Myers, "Eija-Liisa Ahtila: Time Wounds All Heals," *Art/Text* 66 (August–October 1999): 60–64.
9. Magdalena Malm, "The Idea of Linearity Bothers Me: An Interview with Eija-Liisa Ahtila," *Black Box Illuminated*, eds. Sara Arrhenius, Magdalena Malm, and Cristina Ricupero (Stockholm: Propexus, 2003), 74. It is difficult to think about the family relationships in *Me/We* or the unraveling of a marriage in Consolation Services without recalling Ingmar Bergman's 1974 made-for-television series *Scenes from a Marriage.*
10. Daniel Birnbaum, "Crystals of Time: Eija-Liisa Ahtila's Extended Cinema," in *Eija-Liisa Ahtila* (Helsinki: Kiasma Museum of Contemporary Art, 2002), 200; in the same publication, see also Kaja Silverman, "How to Stage the Death of God," 189–195. Exhibition catalogue.
11. Ingmar Bergman, *Images: My Life in Film*, trans. Marianne Ruuth (New York: Arcade Publishing, 1994), 60.
12. Excerpt from the script for *The House*, in *Eija-Liisa Ahtila*, 163.
13. The 1990s saw the setting up of programs that included the Finnish Fund for Art Exchange (FRAME), the Danish Contemporary Art Foundation (DCA), the International Artists Studio Program (IASPIS), and the Nordic Institute for Contemporary Art (NIFCA); see *Nuit blânche: scènes nordiques: les années 90* (Paris: Musée d'Art Moderne de la Ville de Paris, 1998).
14. Cited in Caroline Corbetta, "Master and Servant (About Annika Larsson's Dog)," in *Annika Larsson: Dog* (Salamanca: Centro de Arte de Salamanca, 2000), 5–9. Exhibition catalogue.
15. For an extended discussion of Larsson's choice of masculinity as a subject, see Abigail Solomon-Godeau, "Danger: Men at Work (Or Play)," in *Annika Larsson* (Basel: Museum für Geganwartskunst Basel and Nürnberg: Kunsthalle, 2004), 77–87. Exhibition catalogue.
16. See Håkan Nilsson, "Annika Larsson: Dominance and Submission," *Parkett* 64 (2002): 144–147.
17. Solomon-Godeau notes the similarity between male interaction in Larsson's videos and critic Eve Kosofsky Sedgwick's theorization of what she calls "homosociality," a term that refers to the subtle erotic tension underlying social interactions between men; Solomon-Godeau, *Danger*, 81–82.
18. Interview with the author, New York, June 1, 2005.
19. Raphael Gygax, "The Melody of Loneliness," *Tema Celeste 106* (November–December 2002): 56–59.
20. Michael Wilson, "Jesper Just," *Artforum* (March 2005): 237.

ANNICA KARLSSON RIXON AND ANNIKA LARSSON
ASPECTS OF GENDER AND TRANSNATIONAL POLITICS IN SWEDISH ART

Annika Öhrner

Working from different perspectives and utilizing different artistic strategies, many Scandinavian artists today are posing questions about power and sexuality. And, unlike their counterparts during the emergence of a new avant-garde following World War II, many of them participate actively in a broad international art scene. Annica Karlsson Rixon and Annika Larsson belong to a generation of young Swedish women artists who emerged in the 1990s to establish international careers.[1] *In this essay I address some features of their backgrounds in gender-oriented art and consider some of the related cultural-political strategies implemented by the Swedish government during the past several decades.*

Increasingly we assume that artists worldwide have access to the same visual culture—sharing a common visual archive of images from film, painting, art history, television, the Internet, and photography—in an art world "global village."[2] But is this altogether true? Is it possible perhaps to reconstruct distinct characteristics of a Scandinavian internationalization? Is there a separate, Swedish feminist tradition within the visual arts? Or should we maintain a skeptical attitude to such constructions altogether and investigate political and production-related specifics instead?

We can begin by determining what, from a Swedish perspective, might constitute an international artist in the early postmodern era. In a debate in 1965 in the Swedish daily newspaper *Dagens Nyheter,* the questions of why there were so few such artists and how government policy might change this situation were raised. One contribution to the debate came from a well-informed source. Öyvind Fahlström (1928–1976) had lived in New York since 1961, exhibited at the prestigious Sidney Janis Gallery, and became associated with artists such as Robert Rauschenberg, Claes Oldenburg, and Jean Tinguely. Under the headline "Swedish Art: Honor Guard or Guerrilla?" Fahlström argued that, for an artist to be included in an international context, the artist's work must

> function organically in the international arts world, i.e., in Paris, and particularly in New York. By organic, I mean that there is an unconstrained interplay on all

levels: that the artist receives and gives impulses outside his native country; that he permanently, not just once, is shown by one or more galleries in these cities and that his efforts are considered by critics and essayists; and that his prices keep pace with what the gallery's customer base of collectors and museums pay.... The cultural authorities should be relieved of the responsibility of providing breaches for Swedish art. *No one is interested in Swedishness, on the other hand, the interest is in individual artists.* Equip a guerrilla instead! Quietly drop down a few Swedish artists into the arts jungles of New York, Paris, London and Milan, and let them emerge as a result of what they accomplish and the contacts that they gradually establish when they begin to be able to orient themselves in the sub-vegetation of openings, cafeterias and cocktail bars. Provide them with sufficient grants so that they won't have to rough it, as most of their colleagues, and can give their undivided attention to their art, to receive and give impulses.[3] (author's italics)

The shift of the geographic center of modern art from Paris to New York after World War II had a profound significance for contemporary art. In the early 1980s, art historian Serge Guilbaut challenged the prevailing belief that this was due solely to aesthetic reasons. During the cold war, the United States was able to incorporate the artistic avant-garde into its propaganda promoting American sovereignty. To a certain extent, he argued, American foreign policy could support the new arts and, by doing so, was able to identify the United States with modernity and creativity, while the French government and its museums continued to present earlier modern classics and were ignored. The awarding of the gold medal at the Venice Biennale in 1964 to Robert Rauschenberg has been viewed as the final symbolic victory of New York over Paris.[4]

The transition between the two cities had major consequences for the Swedish arts scene as well. Since the second half of the nineteenth century, waves of Scandinavian artists had gone to Paris to participate in that city's rich vanguard culture in the arts. By the end of the 1950s, international interest had turned to New York. In 1958 the Moderna Museet was founded in Stockholm and, during

Pontus Hultén's leadership at the beginning of the 1960s, American art was introduced in a number of important exhibitions and had a profound effect on the Swedish visual arts.

Despite the impact of American popular and avant-garde culture on that of Scandinavia during this time, few artists from Sweden were given serious attention in America. Some, including Carl Fredrik Reuterswärd, Per Olof Ultvedt, and Barbro Östlihn, enjoyed short-lived success. Swedish-born Claes Oldenburg, who had left Sweden as a child, was hardly part of the Swedish national cultural scene. Despite the exporting of several ambitious and at times successful projects, for several decades there was no Swedish artist who fulfilled Fahlström's 1965 definition of an international artist. Today, Fahlström himself is often portrayed as the first one who did.

Shortly after the extensive debate in *Dagens Nyheter,* responsibility for the internationalization of the contemporary artist became more closely tied to the Moderna Museet's artistic expertise, after having been the responsibility of the Swedish Institute, under the Ministry of Education and Ecclesiastical Affairs. During the following decades, the government committee NUNSKU (the Swedish National Committee for Contemporary Art Exhibitions Abroad) supported or produced Swedish exhibitions abroad. These were directed toward major international arts events and tours in Europe and the Eastern bloc, as well as the United States and, for a few years, even Africa and Asia.[5]

Looking back at the export of Swedish art during the 1960s and 1970s, it is somewhat remarkable that it came almost exclusively from male artists, and not only in prestigious exhibitions. It was of course partly a reflection of the structure of arts in general, Scandinavian as well as North American. Yet the same period witnessed a comparatively progressive gender equality policy in Sweden, though one that obviously did not penetrate to the country's international cultural policy (it goes without saying that Sweden had no lack of significant women artists). After a promising reopening of the Nordic pavilion at the Venice Biennale in 1962 with an installation of the work of the classical modernist and feminist Siri Derkert (1888–1973; together with Per Olof Ultvedt), not until 1995 would biennale audiences encounter a Swedish woman artist in Venice.[6] That year Eva Löfdahl exhibited together with Norway's Per Maning and Finland's Nina Roos.

During the 1970s, a decade marked by a surge of leftist politics, a consciously feminist art movement appeared in Sweden, as in the United States. *Sweden Comes to New York: An Exhibition of Six Women Artists* was shown at the independent A.I.R. (Artists In Residence) Gallery in New York in 1979. Critic Åsa Berntsson chose artists

Grete Billgren, Barbro Bäckström, Kristina Elander, Marie-Louise De Geer Bergenstråhle, Ann-Charlotte Johannesson, and Lenke Rothman.[7] Despite the fact that the exhibit had economic support both from NUNSKU and the National Endowment for the Arts in Washington, D.C., the catalogue bears unfortunate witness to its low budget.

Again during the 1980s, Swedish art was scarcely internationalized, though NUNSKU initiated an exhibition policy in which artists from a younger generation, including women, began to be selected for international representation. NUNSKU was dismantled in 1997, and following a government decision, responsibility for Swedish art abroad was transferred to the Moderna Museet's International Program and to IASPIS (International Artists' Studio Program in Sweden). Both organizations work with the art community and support artists' movement into as well as out of the country.

Today many important Swedish artists live abroad in New York, Berlin or elsewhere, or as nomads in a global village. Some Sweden-based artists can now be considered organically incorporated into the international art world, in Fahlström's definition. There also exists today something that most of Fahlström's generation lacked (though not Fahlström himself): Swedish gallerists with an international orientation, as well as international galleries with an interest in Swedish art.

Swedish art is currently facing new questions about international exchanges. The idea of a "Swedish" art has long been described, by Fahlström and others, as double-edged. It has simultaneously proved to be a useful trademark and an exotic, though less valid, conception. The real question today is whether one can articulate what it means to be a "Swedish artist," especially at a historical moment when Swedes' strong self-perception as egalitarian and tolerant has begun to crack under the strain of implacable statistics from segregated suburbs and inequalities within industry and the workplace.

FEMINIST ARCHAEOLOGY

In the 1970s, the feminist movement encouraged new artistic expression, including the search for a female imagery, the telling of women's lives, and the promotion of textile handicraft as art, as well as important art history projects in which a rewriting of Swedish art history began to take place. All of these issues became part of the cultural arsenal that women artists inherited during the early 1990s, though in my opinion, any aesthetic importance for feminist art in the 1990s was limited.[8]

The most important clues as to why some women artists had an influence during the 1990s—at home and later internationally—are not to be found in cultural policy, but in other developments in Swedish art. A countermovement against the dominant field of emphatic documentary photography, in which Christer Strömholm

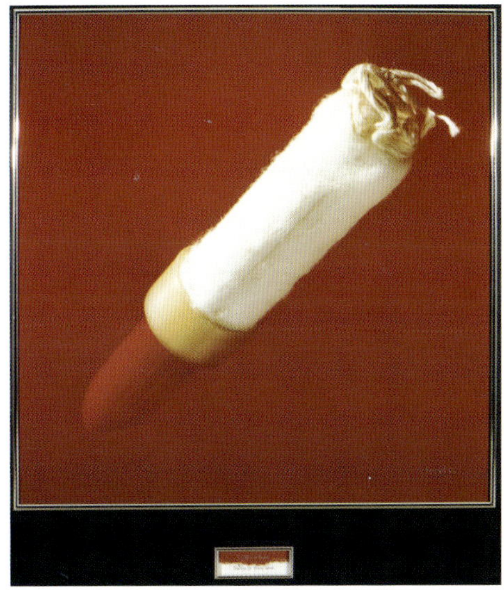

Ingrid Orfali, *La Chute d'Ariane*, 1986
C print
39.4 x 39.4 in. (101 x 101 cm) (image)
Collection of the Moderna Museet, Stockholm

was a leading figure, coincided with the influence of continental and American postmodern theory and opened up entirely new aesthetic attitudes. This can be observed, for example, in the works of two artists, Ingrid Orfali (b. 1952) and Tuija Lindström (b. 1950).

Ingrid Orfali exhibited in Sweden from the middle of the 1980s to about 1990. Her spare, photo-based images show selected objects against intense monochrome surfaces, invoking the formal language of advertising. Highly charged visually, they were effective in their subversive use of symbols. Orfali had a significant relationship to surrealist image traditions, and her works were created from a linguistic-philosophical perspective in which titles were an important component. In a text about her relationship to the concept of the "copy," she states that the copy cannot come about without a distortion of the original and that it does not necessarily originate from an image. "A photograph can be a copy of a word, a sentence, a sound, a myth etc."[9] With roots in French semiotics, she created an image world that became a visual harbinger of ideas from central European culture and philosophers such as Jacques Lacan and Julia Kristeva. Orfali's images radically challenged the prevailing Swedish modernist painterly tradition. The fact that, in addition, several of the images engaged with "queer" content was something that not all critics were able to address.

Orfali's presence on the Swedish arts scene coincided with an emerging American postmodern discourse that spread throughout the Western world. In Sweden it landed in the midst of a domestic discussion about photography as art or document, a discussion that for some years was highly charged and far-ranging. It is impossible to overestimate the importance of American postmodern photography for Swedish photo-based art of the 1990s. It was conveyed in various ways through magazines and electronic media, and a broad breakthrough occurred when Lars Nittve organized the exhibition *Implosion* at the Moderna Museet in 1987. During that fall, a major debate about the validity of the concept for Swedish art had already been initiated by critic Lars O. Ericsson, who was instrumental in spreading the new concept beyond narrow academic circles. An issue of Fotograficentrum's magazine *Bildtidningen* (no. 4, 1990) became a milestone for the introduction of feminist photo-based art from the United States to younger artists in Sweden.[10] In that issue, concepts such as deconstruction, originality, and the male gaze were analyzed, and works by Laurie Simmons, Barbara Kruger, Cindy Sherman, and Mary Kelly, among others, were reproduced. Postmodern feminism quickly became one of the current tendencies diligently studied in art schools, not the least being University College of Arts, Craft and Design in Stockholm, where several of the feminist artists of the 1990s studied.[11]

The works of Tuija Lindström had very different origins from those of Orfali. Lindström, who received her education in the Department of Photography at the University College of Arts, Craft and Design, had also been a student of Christer Strömholm. She became an important presence by the early 1980s, a period otherwise characterized by discord in the realm of photography, notably between the perception of the photograph's function as aesthetic object or document.[12] Her influential work *Kvinnorna vid Tjursjön* (The Girls at Bull's Pond; 1991–92) is central to an understanding of her strategies. It consists of a series of images, mainly black-and-white and printed in large format, and a 16mm black-and-white film. Dreamlike and sensual images of white female bodies floating in water were combined with large images of clothing irons, one of which was smeared with blood. The images simultaneously evoke an enigmatic, female subjectivity and pleasurable awareness of the body, as well as constructs of violence and acts of cruelty. Lindström's work radically broke both with the tradition of painterly modernism that somehow dominated the Swedish art world and with the photographic tradition from which she herself came. In 1992, Lindström was appointed professor at *Högskolan för Fotografi* (College of Photography) at Gothenburg University, where she stayed until 2002. She has been of major importance to a younger generation.

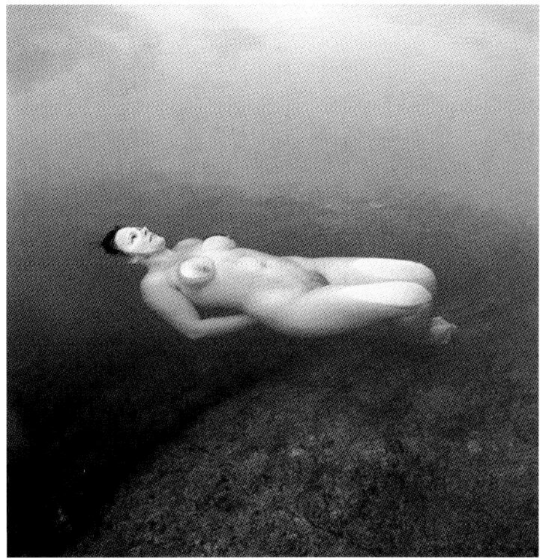

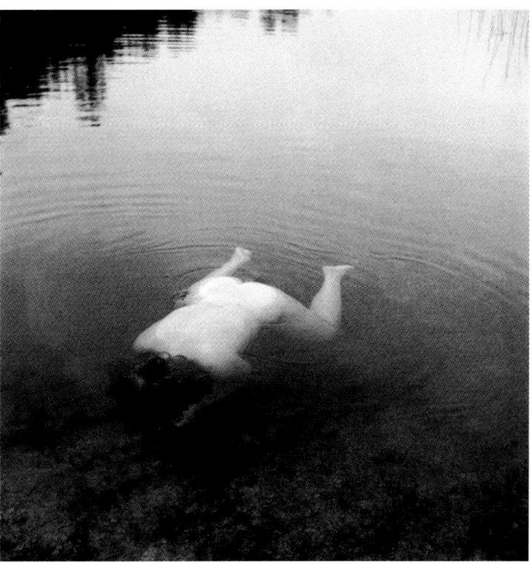

Tuija Lindström, *The Girls at Bull's Pond*, 1991–92
Gelatin silver prints
Each 23.4 x 23.4 in. (60 x 60 cm)
Courtesy of the artist

Thus it might be argued that the importance of the photographic medium for postmodern feminist art coincides temporally with the definitive breakthrough of the art of photography. During the 1990s, an unusually strong generation of Swedish women artists emerged to make their mark in the international art world. The two Swedish artists in the exhibition *BENT: Gender and Sexuality in Contemporary Scandinavian Art*, Annica Karlsson Rixon and Annika Larsson, are part of this phenomenon. Their artistic careers began a few years apart, however, and are profoundly distinct. Like Jesper Just and Eija-Liisa Ahtila, they relate to the visual culture Whitney Chadwick discusses in her essay in this catalogue. Here I would like to isolate two issues relevant to Karlsson Rixon's and Larsson's work: the ways in which they address questions of gender and the importance of their transnational methods of working.

TRANSGRESSION AND CONQUEST

Annica Karlsson Rixon's (b. 1962) debut at Fotocentrum's gallery in Stockholm in 1991 consisted of a series of six color photographs, *Untitled I–VI* (1990). Four of the images depict a female torso in a classical pose positioned against a blue background. An image of an animal or a plant has been superimposed on each torso. In one, a large calla lily placed in front of the womb creates an ambiguous, phallic expression; in

Left to right:
Annica Karlsson Rixon, *Untitled I–VI*, 1990
C prints
Each 15 x 15 in. (38.1 x 38.1 cm)
Courtesy of the artist

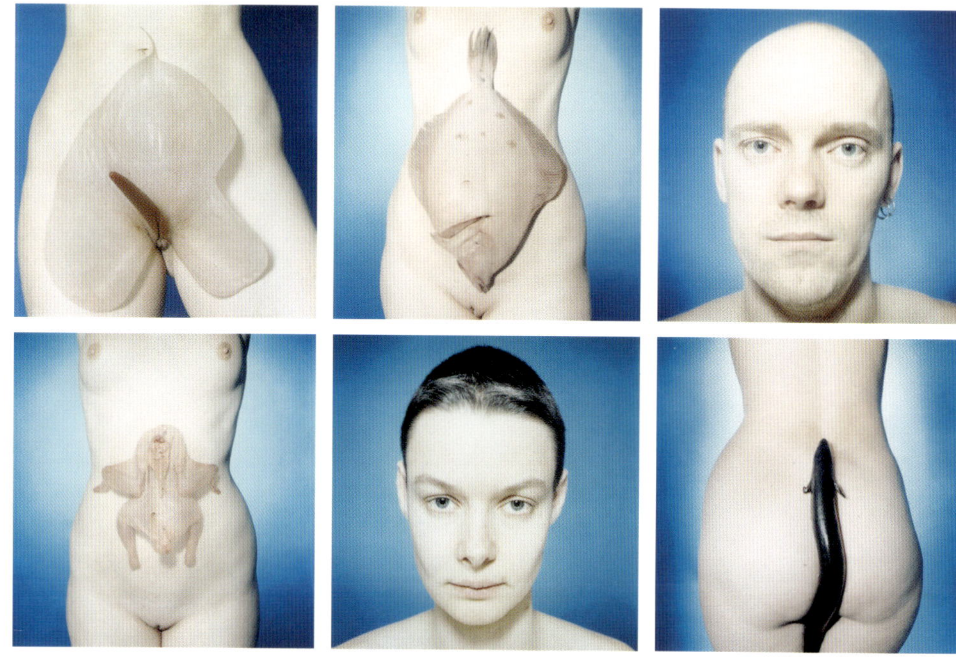

another, a black eel seems to slide erotically across the body. The series also contains images of a raw flounder and a plucked chicken lying against the stomach of the model, suggesting pregnancies. The cold slimy surfaces and their secondary status as foodstuff create tactile and oral associations, and challenge the integrity of the body. Two images in the series, however, differ from the others. These are frontal, artless portraits of a woman and a man whose facial features and short shaved hair emphasize their similarity. The facial features are pale and vacant, except for the gazes, which are intense and directed toward the viewer. *Untitled I–VI* is charged with powerful and complex desires, contradictory bodily experiences, and ambiguous sexual identity while invoking surrealism through the juxtaposition of unrelated objects.

The series had a strong influence and became the prelude to Karlsson Rixon's subsequent work in which she would continue to address gender issues, though with less evident surrealist influence. The foundation of her work remained a strong and technically focused relationship to the photograph as genre. Using carefully selected formats, she has explored a variety of approaches that interrogate aspects of male-dominated and heteronormative image traditions and realities. For the series *Truckers & Others* (1998–99), she photographed male truckers waving as they passed her on California freeways. Their stereotypical gestures have been isolated and variously

Opposite page, top to bottom:

Annica Karlsson Rixon, *Ingeborg and Fanny, Fatima and Olle, Leif and Carlmichael, Marita and Kristofer* from the series *Stockholm 2 Close*, 2002
C prints
Each 11.3 x 12.9 in. (29 x 33 cm)
Courtesy of the artist

grouped in taut, repetitive arrangements and hung together with monochrome color prints. The monochromes signify evasive and faceless objects that are the precondition of the gesture and, at the same time, provide a sharp aesthetic contrast to the "documentary look" of the gestures.

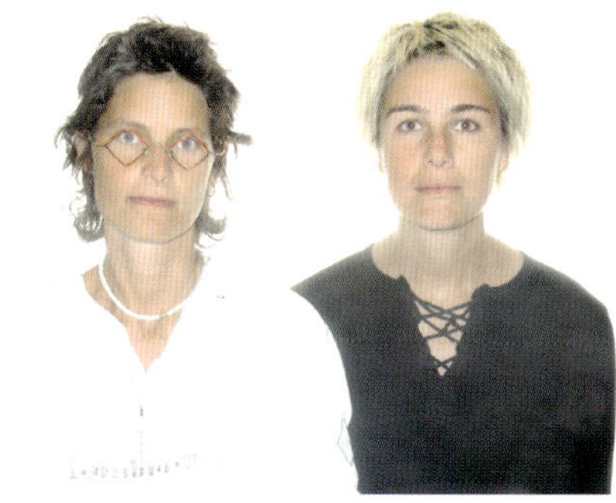

During the past ten years, Karlsson Rixon has also turned to portraiture. In the series *Portraits in Nordic Light* (1997–98), *Stockholm 2 Close* (2002), and *Annika by the Sea* (1999–2001), and in an ongoing work titled *Resonance,* she plays with the discursive limits of portraiture. Between 1994 and 1999, Karlsson Rixon lived in southern California. Around the same time, Scandinavian painting from the late nineteenth and early twentieth centuries was appearing in large exhibitions in the United States and Europe, many of which bore titles that resurrected the idea of a unique Nordic light. Many of these paintings depict light-infused romantic artistic milieus in Paris, Danish Skagen, and the Swedish countryside, painted during the last decades of the nineteenth century. The paintings, which often focus on artistic fellowship, male creativity, quiet intimacy, and melancholy love, are frequently based on photographs.

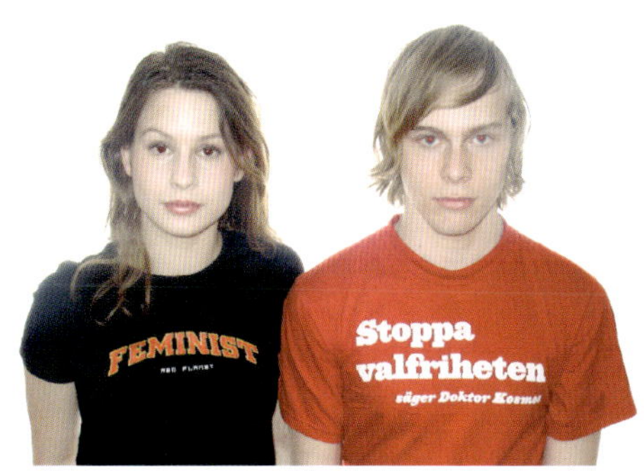

Today such pictures are a familiar part of the collective Scandinavian artistic heritage, appearing not only in museums but also in popular culture, in feature films, on posters and placemats. To Scandinavian artists of today, they often seem irrevocably exhausted from overuse. During her self-imposed exile, Karlsson Rixon began to see them from a different perspective. In the project *Portraits in Nordic Light,* she used some of the most familiar of these paintings as sources for large-format color images. Her versions re-create their sources' effects of light and register each minute shift in milieus and faces, but with a strong photographic expression. In them Karlsson Rixon also re-creates the artistic milieu of her own generation—its friendships, social gatherings, and love affairs. *Portraits in Nordic Light* exposes the assumptions underlying the perception of gender equality and the myth of male creativity often perceived in the paintings on which they are based, paintings that have assumed canonical status. Equally important is the fact that these photographs tell a new story, one based on the artist's own context.[13]

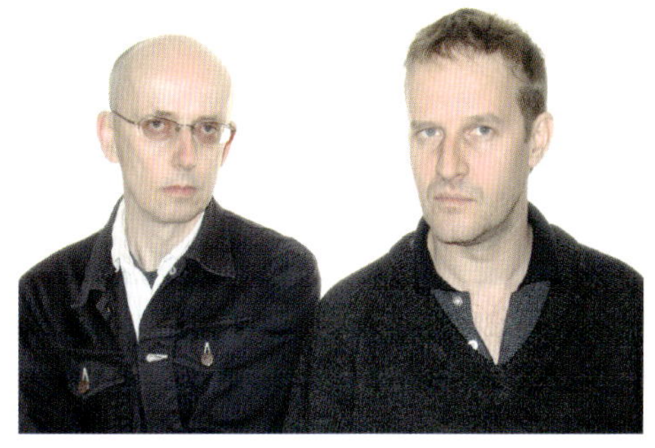

The series *Annika by the Sea* is an independent continuation of the project initiated with *Portraits in Nordic Light.* By this time Karlsson Rixon had returned to Sweden and discovered that her friends and peers had assumed positions in the contemporary art world. She decided to initiate a large portrait project, inspired by a painting from Skagen by Peder Severin Krøyer, *Summer Evening at Skagen Beach* (1892). The series consists of photographs of female figures standing on beaches at different oceans in the world. It can also be seen as a commentary on historical portraiture of male heroes.

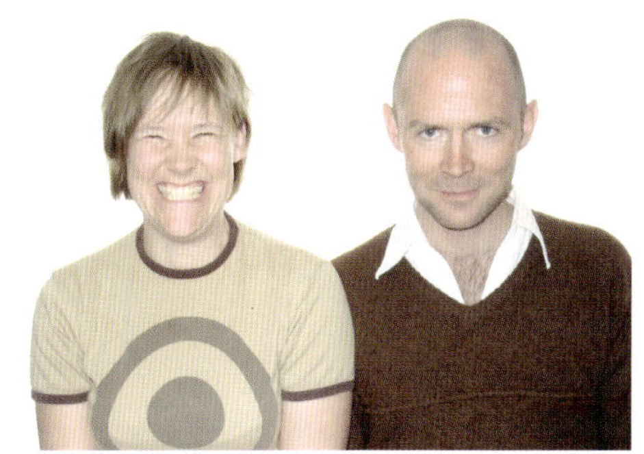

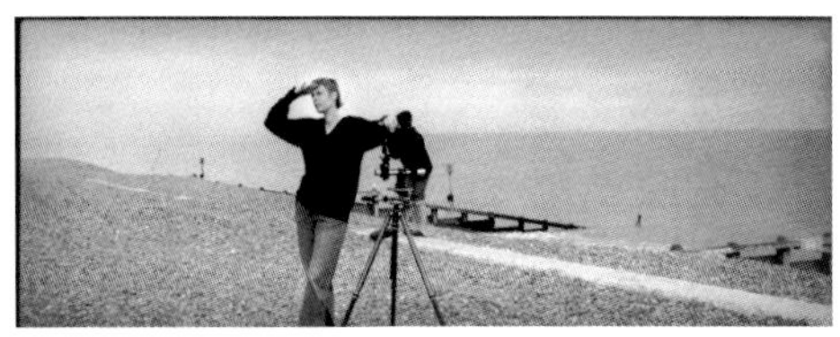

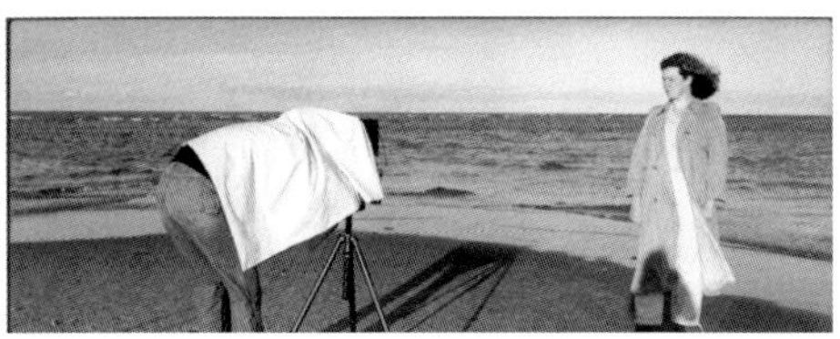

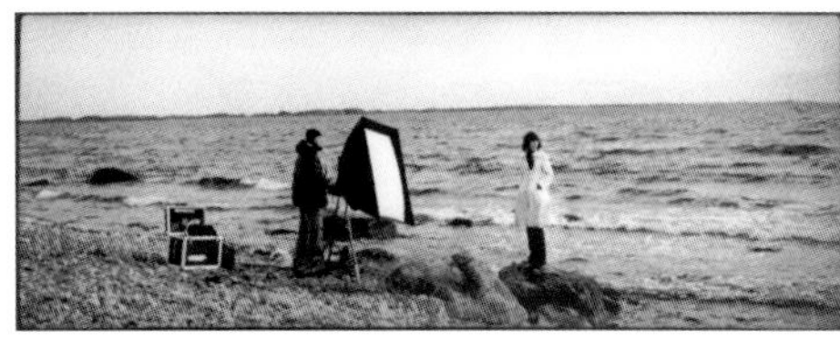

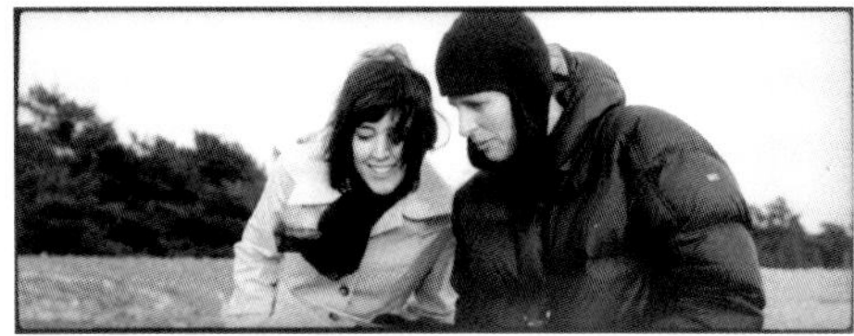

Top to bottom:

Marit Jacobsen, *Annica Karlsson Rixon looking for the light,* 2000
Black-and-white photograph
10.5 x 18.3 in. (27 x 47 cm)
Courtesy of the artist

Evelina Gustavsson, *Annica Karlsson Rixon and Annika Öhrner,* 2000
Black-and-white photograph
10.5 x 18.3 in. (27 x 47 cm)
Courtesy of the artist

Pernilla Zetterman, *Annica Karlsson Rixon and Annika Larsson,* 2000
Black-and-white photograph
10.5 x 18.3 in. (27 x 47 cm)
Courtesy of the artist

Pernilla Zetterman, *Annika Larsson and Annica Karlsson Rixon,* 2000
Black-and-white photograph
10.5 x 18.3 in. (27 x 47 cm)
Courtesy of the artist

With *Annika by the Sea,* Karlsson Rixon also deliberately constructs a female network that operates both symbolically and factually. Such a network challenges a system in which men have often formed themselves into instinctive or organized gender-based networks. Here Karlsson Rixon also seems to suggest that organization by gender is as arbitrary a means of selection as any other. The project involved a large group of individuals and extensive travel to seaside locations, during which new constellations, contacts, and exchanges emerged. Karlsson Rixon also included young female art students as assistants, thereby bringing them into the process. It is also possible to view *Annika by the Sea* as an artistic interpretation of the phenomenon of the transnational feminism we are discussing here.

The female models were placed on ocean beaches in various locations and photographed in both color and black-and-white using a box camera with all its implications of theatrical presentation. All the models are named Annika: Annica Karlsson Rixon herself, Annika Larsson, Annika Eriksson, Annika von Hausswolff, Annika Lundgren, Annika Ström, and Annika Öhrner.[14] Annika is a common name in the Swedish generation born in the 1960s or early 1970s and signaled normalcy through its identification with Pippi Longstocking's well-behaved friend Annika in Astrid Lindgren's widely read stories.

Karlsson Rixon's portrait photographs deconstruct various modernistic and masculinist traditions in art history, artistic practices, and documentary photography. Appropriating the dominant paradigm, she interpolates a different gender order, which simultaneously reveals and communicates a possible alternative. The directness and the indexical nature of the photograph are basic to and productive of such a strategy.

NORMALCY MEDIATED

Annika Larsson (b. 1972) had worked extensively in painting and drawing at preparatory art schools before she was admitted to the Royal College of Art in Stockholm in 1995. For two years she studied at the school's computer department, browsed the Internet, and downloaded online images. Today she believes that the encounter with video art and conceptual, anti-aesthetic contemporary art was crucial for her emerging practice.[15] Her first video work, *Inbjudan till Herr B* (Invitation to Mr. B; 1998), was created while she was still a student and used amateur actors staged in stereotypically male interactions. The same year she was chosen to film a performance by Vanessa Beecroft in the exhibit *Wounds: Between Democracy and Redemption in Contemporary Art* at the Moderna Museet in Stockholm. In Beecroft's performance (VB34), a group of interchangable female models wandered around in high heels and black hats in the museum's entry hall. Now and then they stopped and posed, one of them holding an American flag in her hand. Larsson's documentation of Beecroft's performance in Stockholm led to further collaboration between the two artists.

Larsson's films have a spare and pure aesthetic that extends beyond the purely pictorial. The soundtracks, frequently produced in cooperation with musician, performance artist, and partner Tobias Bernstrup, contribute to this aesthetic. Her works are presented as large video projections in darkened rooms, sometimes accessible only through a single door, which is closed behind the visitor. They are peopled with protagonists, or with a subject and object of desire, but these roles are often ambiguous and the actions without an obvious direction. Because of the works' nonnarrative nature, observers are drawn into them in an attempt to provide meaning, to understand the origin of the danger or the target of the desire.

Beginning with the earliest video works, Larsson's actors performed what seem like ritual acts. These actions, stereotypically male or apparently meaningless and repetitive, create a powerful, suppressed tension in the visual presentation. Several of Larsson's works also depict institutional or terrorist violence. In *D.I.E.* (2000), men are executed in a closed room; in *Poliisi* (2001), a group of policemen resort to the use of truncheons. In *Bend II* (2002), the violence is exercised in a power play that develops between a male actor and his avatar in the interface between cyberspace and reality. The violence in Larsson's works is almost always fictitiously presented but appears highly realistic.

Larsson's book *Diary #2* offers a straightforward narrative of a visual practice in which the computer serves as an endless resource, but also as the central workplace.[16] As Larsson wrote to Vanessa Beecroft in an e-mail dialogue published in *Diary #2*, "Almost all my life is in front of or inside of a computer. Outside is too slow." In this cyberspace she determines the visual components of the work, creates an idea about environment, searches for it in the physical world, and samples appearances, structures, and characters from different spheres. In *Pink Ball* (2002), which is featured in *Diary #2*, the collecting takes place within realms of social meaning including physical therapy, nudism, sports, and pornography.

Two aspects are essential to understanding how gender and identity operate in Larsson's work. The first is her method of working. Early in her artistic career she immersed herself in early video art. Later, living in Berlin, she studied other types of moving images, including early German propaganda films. The collecting of visual material, however, takes place primarily in the digital space, from where she downloads the pictures she finds of interest. Out of this archive of fragments from a collective

GENDER AND SEX IN SCANDINAVIAN CINEMA AS SCREENED IN THE AMERICAN MIND

Linda Haverty Rugg

The worldwide association of Scandinavia with uninhibited sex springs largely from representations of gender and sex in Nordic films, beginning already in the silent era. Typical traces of this phenomenon in American culture can be found in the B-grade Bob Hope comedy *I'll Take Sweden* ("ja, ja, ja!"; 1965) with its scantily clad, bed-hopping blondes; the Swedish Bikini Team's *Never Say Never Mind* (2002); and soft porn such as *Swedish Fly Girls* (1971) with its promotional line, "Every man should meet a free-flying stewardess once in his lifetime. Fly girls who know what to do for and to a man." Scandinavian filmmakers have played consciously with the image of Scandinavian women, framing them as natural creatures, sexually liberated within the backdrop of a sensual Scandinavian summer.

At the same time, an associated Scandinavian cinematic tradition of asserting the strength of women and the centrality of female experience has contributed to the popular image of the Valkyrie,[1] or in more mundane terms, the Scandinavian Mama who rules the household, lovingly but forcefully pushing her effeminized mate to the side. Americans have reproduced this stereotype in the film and television series *I Remember Mama* (1948 and 1949–62, respectively), in the (arguably) feminist political comedy *The Farmer's Daughter* (1948), and in numerous Westerns such as John Ford's *The Searchers* (1956) and *The Man Who Shot Liberty Valance* (1962).[2]

A less obvious type emerges as an outgrowth of the combination between sex object and Valkyrie: the martyr. Women in Scandinavian cinema who assert themselves through sexual self-determination or other independent action often find themselves the victims of patriarchy's wrath, as in Victor Sjöström's *The Wind* or *The Scarlet Letter,* Carl Dreyer's *Passion of Joan of Arc,* Ingmar Bergman's *The Seventh Seal,* or Lars von Trier's *Dancer in the Dark.* The pattern emerges with sufficient frequency and centrality to raise questions about attitudes in progressive Scandinavia regarding sexual freedom and the status of women.

The Nordic bent in gender representation appears at the birth of narrative cinematic history. One of the most notorious early shorts was Mrs. Anna Larssen in *Her Dressing-Room* (1901, Peter Elfelt). Typical of the "cinema of attractions" of the period,[3] the short features a celebrated Danish actress taking off her costume after a performance.

Just as she approaches the revelation of forbidden charms, the film action ends and is reversed, so that she is "magically" dressed again.[4] The use of the cinematic medium to intrude upon a private space, in particular a feminine space imbued with sexual connotation, speaks to this early director's understanding of the voyeuristic erotic possibilities inherent in the technology. If Anna Larssen in her dressing room can be taken as a forerunner to the eroticized Nordic woman of later periods, we can see one of the cinematic Ur-Valkyries in *The Robber's Bride* (1907, Viggo Larsen). This film plays out in an unspecified milieu with hints of a Wild West setting, but it is distinguished by its strong and active heroine, whose inept robber-mate requires her constant assistance, startlingly like the Scandinavian couples' dynamic in the Westerns of John Ford.

While the early dressing room short is not peculiarly Scandinavian, it seems significant that Copenhagen's Nordisk Films Kompagni (founded 1906) based its first full feature on a highly successful mix of moral pedagogy and sexploitation, *The White Slave Trade* (1910, August Blom). The tendency to focus on the exotically erotic characterized the early films of Nordisk, which ranked third in size among the world's producers in 1913 and was strong internationally throughout the pre–World War I era. The first European film diva, Asta Nielsen, got her start performing the sexually daring "Gaucho Dance" in the popular Nordisk production *The Abyss* (1910, Urban Gad). Nielsen's relatively dark, "exotic" appearance ensured her reception as a sexualized temptress, a role that Greta Garbo would later perform in Hollywood.

Sweden in the meantime attempted to "elevate" the cinema of attractions. *Svenska Bio* (Swedish Film, founded 1907) made a conscious effort to yoke film with literature, in part in reaction to the eroticism and violence of early cinema. The author of choice for film adaptations was Selma Lagerlöf, one of Sweden's best-known cultural personalities. Eleven silent films were based on her works, several of them masterpieces of early Swedish film, in part because they were made by the two greatest directors of the Swedish silent period, Victor Sjöström and Mauritz Stiller. That Lagerlöf's work is feminist in a modern sense is debatable, but it is clear that the decision to focus on her work produced a very different image of Scandinavian women and sexuality. Her heroines as filmed by Sjöström and Stiller occupy positions of strength and power, tending

Urban Gad, *The Abyss*, 1910
Danish Film Institute, Image and Poster Archive

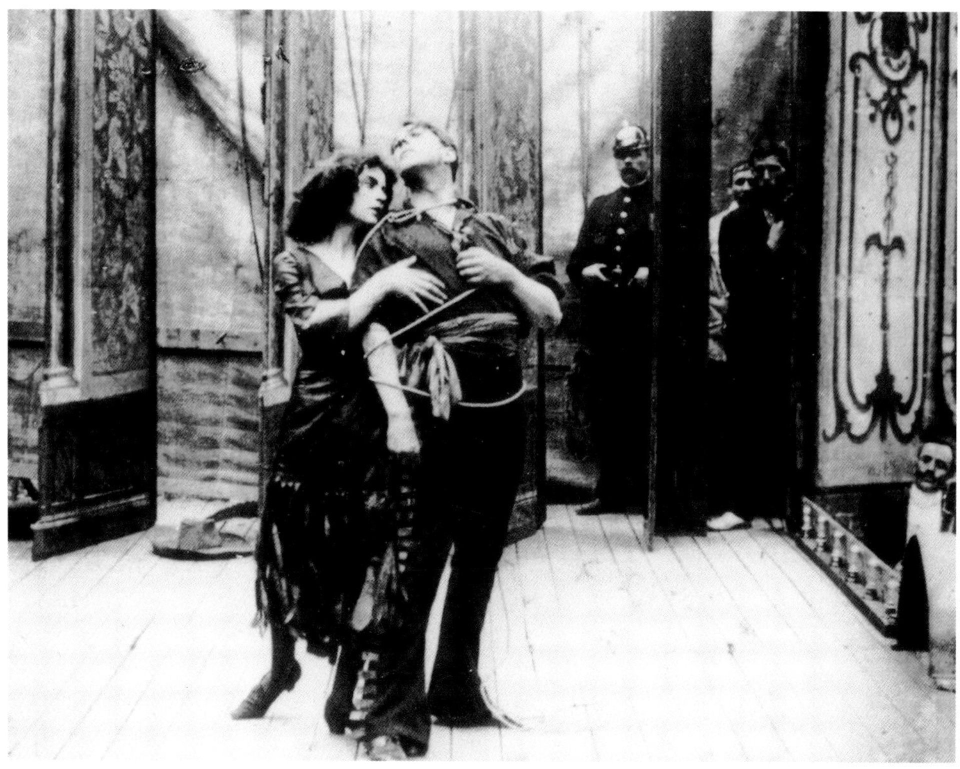

in some cases to reproduce the Valkyrie stereotype. An exception might be Greta Garbo in *The Saga of Gösta Berling* (1924, Mauritz Stiller). Here Garbo is, like Asta Nielsen and other early stars, a "foreigner," an Italian countess who falls fatefully in love with the saga's hero.

Garbo's career opens another era of the representation of Scandinavian gender and sexuality. After the international success of *Gösta Berling*, the director, Mauritz Stiller, was courted by Hollywood, and he brought his young star along. Garbo quickly achieved fame as the silent, sultry heroine of films such as *Flesh and the Devil* (1926) and *A Woman of Affairs* (1928). Clearly the Scandinavian reputation for eroticism survived the Atlantic crossing, despite or perhaps because of the peculiar frigidity in the pristine lines of Garbo's face that overlay a presumably volcanic interior.

In 1923 Victor Sjöström also arrived in Hollywood. He imported a particular representation of women as victimized (and sexualized) yet strong. The best American examples of this exist in two extraordinary silent films, *The Scarlet Letter* (1926) and *The Wind* (1928). Lillian Gish, already an established silent film screen star, requested to work on these projects with Sjöström and his Swedish leading actor, Lars Hanson.

Both of these films provide an opportunity for Gish to dominate the screen as a woman battling indomitable forces yet exuding tremendous strength and sensuality. Garbo's successor of the 1940s, Ingrid Bergman, occupies a similar role in such films as *Casablanca* (1942), *Gaslight* (1944), *Spellbound* (1945), and *Notorious* (1946), but her roles tend to cast her in a more vulnerable position. Nevertheless, the camera makes a study of her face in much the same way it reflects upon Garbo's, using lighting and close-ups to produce the notion of an absolute "feminine beauty" with a racialized cast.

A new wave of associations between Scandinavia and sex emerged in the 1950s with the postwar importation of films from Sweden. It was at this moment, when Scandinavia really became synonymous with soft porn, that Ingmar Bergman entered the American scene. His early European success *Monika* (1953) played in the United States as *Monika: The Story of a Bad Girl.* Woody Allen describes the moment: "I was a teenager living in Brooklyn, and word got out that there was a Swedish film coming to our local film house in which a young woman swam completely naked." Although he admits that he paid little attention to the beauty of the cinematography, he later realized that "it was my first exposure to a director who I would come to believe was pound for pound the best of all filmmakers."[5] *Monika* was distributed in the United States at theaters that trafficked in soft porn, and several were prosecuted for showing the film.

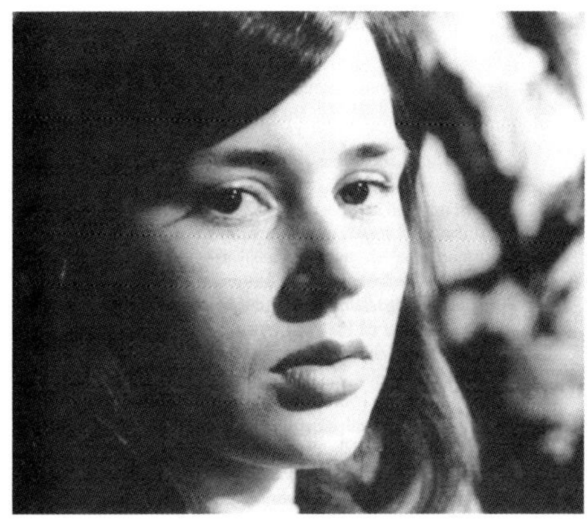

Ingmar Bergman, *Monika*, 1953
©AB Svensk Filmindustri
Photo: Louis Huch

Allen's dual recognition of Bergman as an artist and a producer of erotic images was typical. Bergman's initial success abroad rested on his naturalistic representation of sexuality, usually female sexuality, expressed, however, in highly artistic terms. This was not the soft porn Woody Allen expected as a teen, but a new approach to dealing with sex and gender, influenced in part by the more open Scandinavian cultural attitude toward nudity and sexuality, the tendency in Scandinavia to censor for violence rather than sex, and the legalization of pornography in Scandinavia.

As Bergman's career progressed and the art cinema movement burgeoned, he moved from framing women within the sensuous backdrop of the Swedish summer to plumbing the dark spaces of the psyche, still concentrating, however, on women and their sexuality. Films such as *The Silence* (1963), which deals with masturbation, incest, frigidity, and nymphomania, *Persona* (1966), and *Cries and Whispers* (1968) focus tightly on an agonized vision of women entrapped in essentializing constructions of gender: motherhood, caretaking, repressed sexuality, and subordination in marriage. The contemporary American reception of the films saw the focus on sex but tended to miss the feminist critique; a *Playboy* interview with Bergman in 1964 observes: "most of [the audience] comes to ogle the most explicitly erotic movie scenes on view this side of a stag smoker."[6]

Another transatlantic confusion occurred in conjunction with the release of Vilgot Sjöman's *I Am Curious: Yellow* in 1967. Sjöman's film was confiscated by the American authorities for its "obscene" content: nude sexual intercourse and scenes involving oral sex. The judges in the appellate court understood upon viewing the film that the film was not intended as sexual titillation. Sjöman's film is in fact a self-reflexive, ingenious, and hilarious parody of social experimentation in Sweden. Nevertheless, because it was marketed in conjunction with a book published by Grove Press including explicit photographs from the film, audiences lined up for an erotic extravaganza. But those expecting a sensual experience were disappointed. What should have struck viewers instead was the young woman at the film's center, Lena Nyman, who sets out on her own to challenge the sterility of Swedish socialist bureaucracy. Lena offers a wonderful combination of the Valkyrie and the eroticized Scandinavian with a mind of her own. But perhaps because of Lena's youthful insouciance and sexualization, few recognize the film as a feminist statement.

As we entered the new millennium, Danish director Lars von Trier produced films in the tradition of Carl Dreyer's *Passion of Joan of Arc* (1928). Like Dreyer, von Trier focuses on the martyred, even sadistically tortured, woman. His *Breaking the Waves* (1996), *Dancer in the Dark* (2000), and *Dogville* (2003) all feature heroines who undergo exquisite agony of a sexual and/or emotional nature. Many spectators experience an intense level of discomfort in watching the spectacle of the woman's pain. Yet there are moments in each case where the woman seems unconquerable, either through her access to spiritual or imaginative escape or through acts of revenge. In von Trier's work (as in Sjöström's American films) the action occurs outside Scandinavia, but the women still exude the qualities of strength that mark the Valkyrie stereotype.

A number of forces in cinematic history—political, economic, cultural, and aesthetic—conjoined to construct an international image of Scandinavian women as sexually liberated and threateningly autonomous (and thus in some cases slated for martyrdom). Further, cultural and political differences in the countries of origin and the countries of distribution contrived to create confusion. When Scandinavian women travel abroad, they experience the real effects of the cinematic stereotypes. It remains to be seen how the present globalization of film, with its multinational production companies, will transform the national and regional aspects of gender construction and sexual identity.

NOTES

1. Valkyries were mythic women who served the god Odin on the battlefield. The name means literally "chooser of the slain," and it was the belief of pagan Scandinavians that men who died in battle would be "chosen" and flown to the warrior's paradise Valhalla by these armored maidens. The most popular representation of the Valkyrie figure exists in Richard Wagner's version of Brunhilde, the massive, breast-plated warrior woman.

2. Both Ford films feature the character actor John Qualen as the apron-wearing Swedish Papa; Qualen made a virtual career of this gender-bending stereotype.

3. This term was coined by film scholar Tom Gunning to describe the early development of cinema, particularly the short variety film, in relation to earlier forms of visual culture rather than literary narrative, and new experiences of space and time in modernity. See "The Cinema of Attractions: Early Film, Its Spectator and the Avant-Garde," in *Early Film,* ed. Thomas Elsaesser and Adam Barker (British Film Institute, 1989).

4. Described in Casper Tybjerg, *100 Års Dansk Film,* ed. Peter Schepelern (Copenhagen: Rosinante, 2001), 17.

5. Woody Allen, "Through a Life Darkly," in *Ingmar Bergman: An Artist's Journey*, ed. Roger W. Oliver (New York: Arcade, 1995), 25–26.

6. "Interview with Ingmar Bergman," *Playboy* (June 1964): 61.

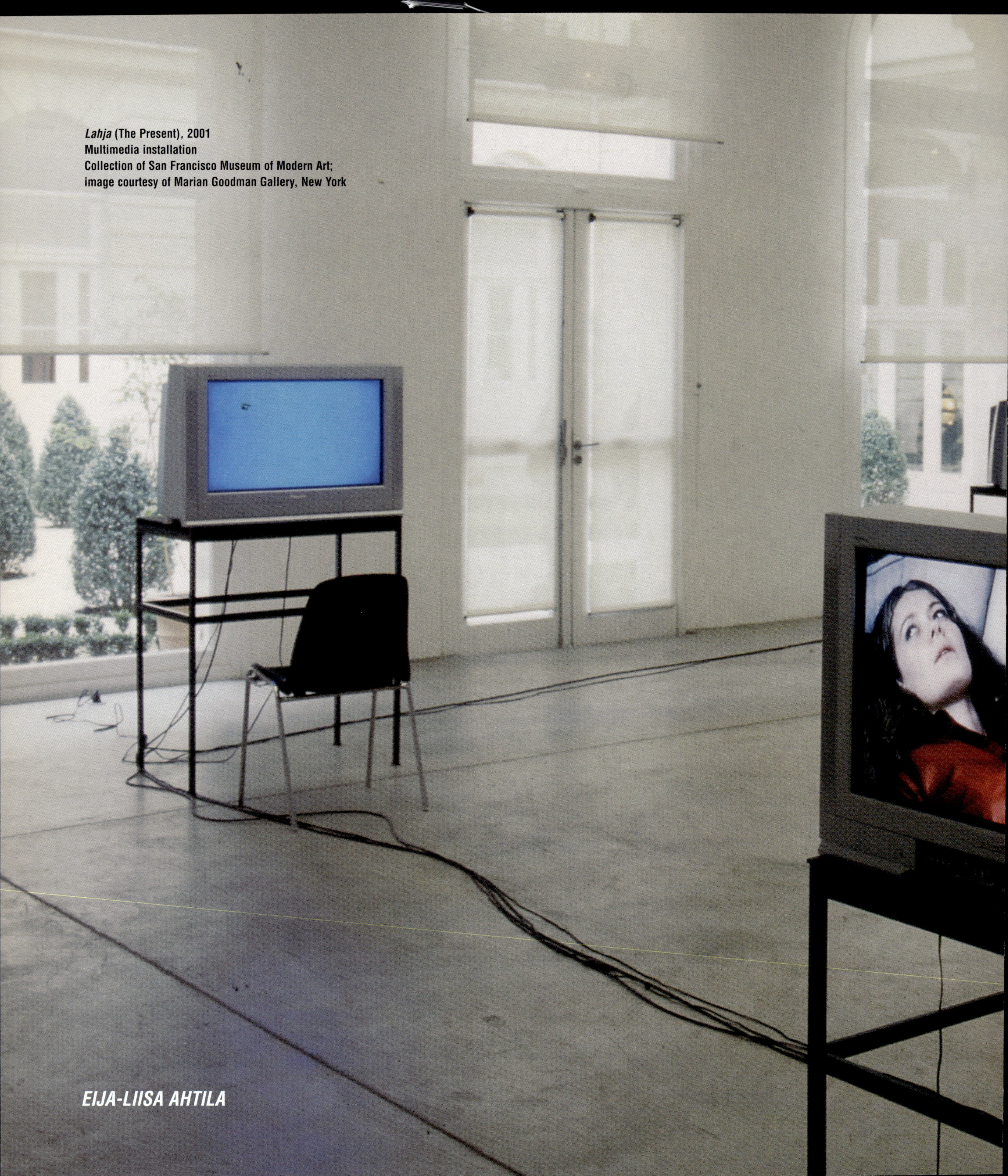

Lahja (The Present), 2001
Multimedia installation
Collection of San Francisco Museum of Modern Art;
image courtesy of Marian Goodman Gallery, New York

EIJA-LIISA AHTILA

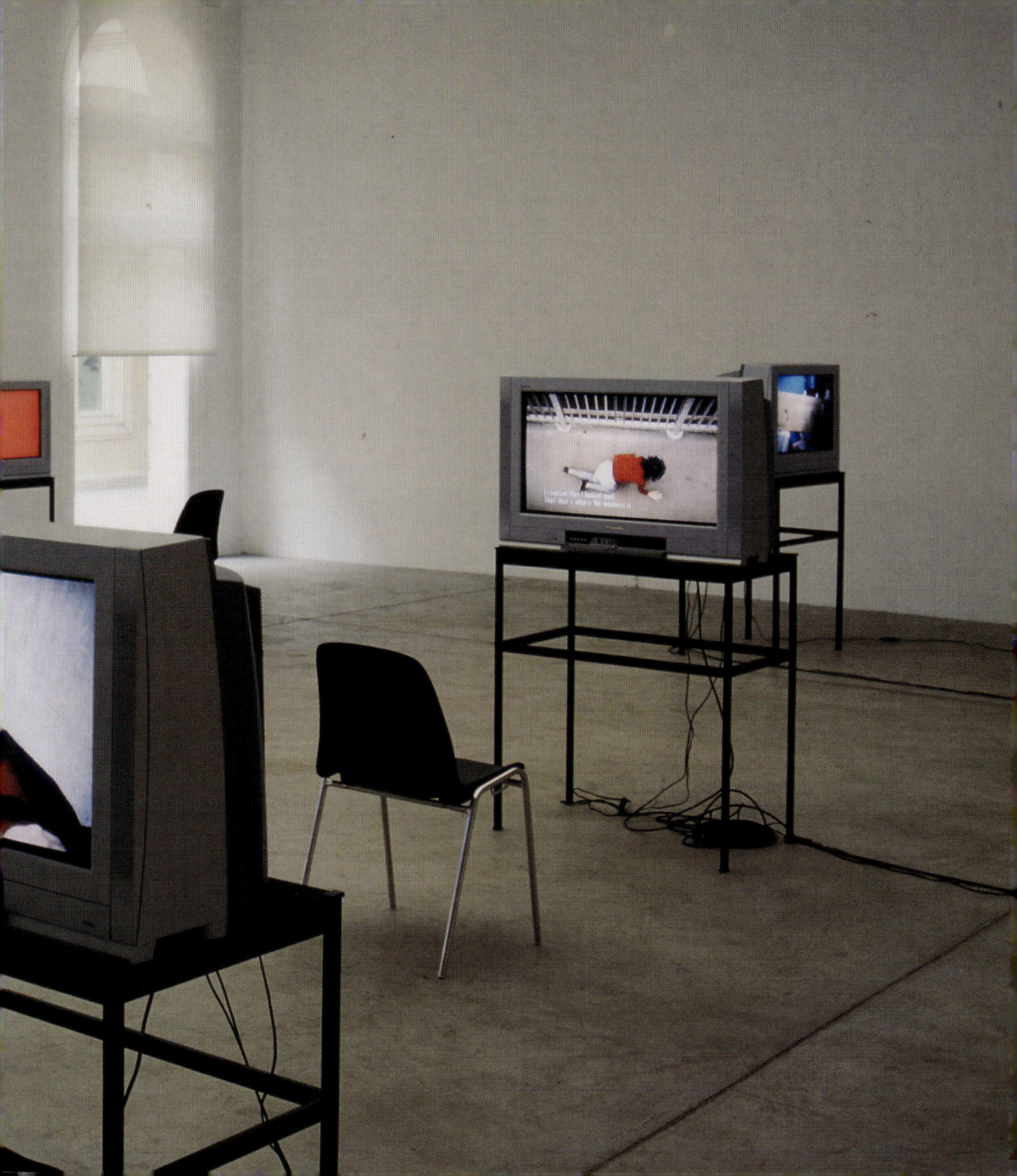

Still from *The House*, 2002
DVD multiscreen installation, 14:00 minutes
Courtesy of Marian Goodman Gallery, New York

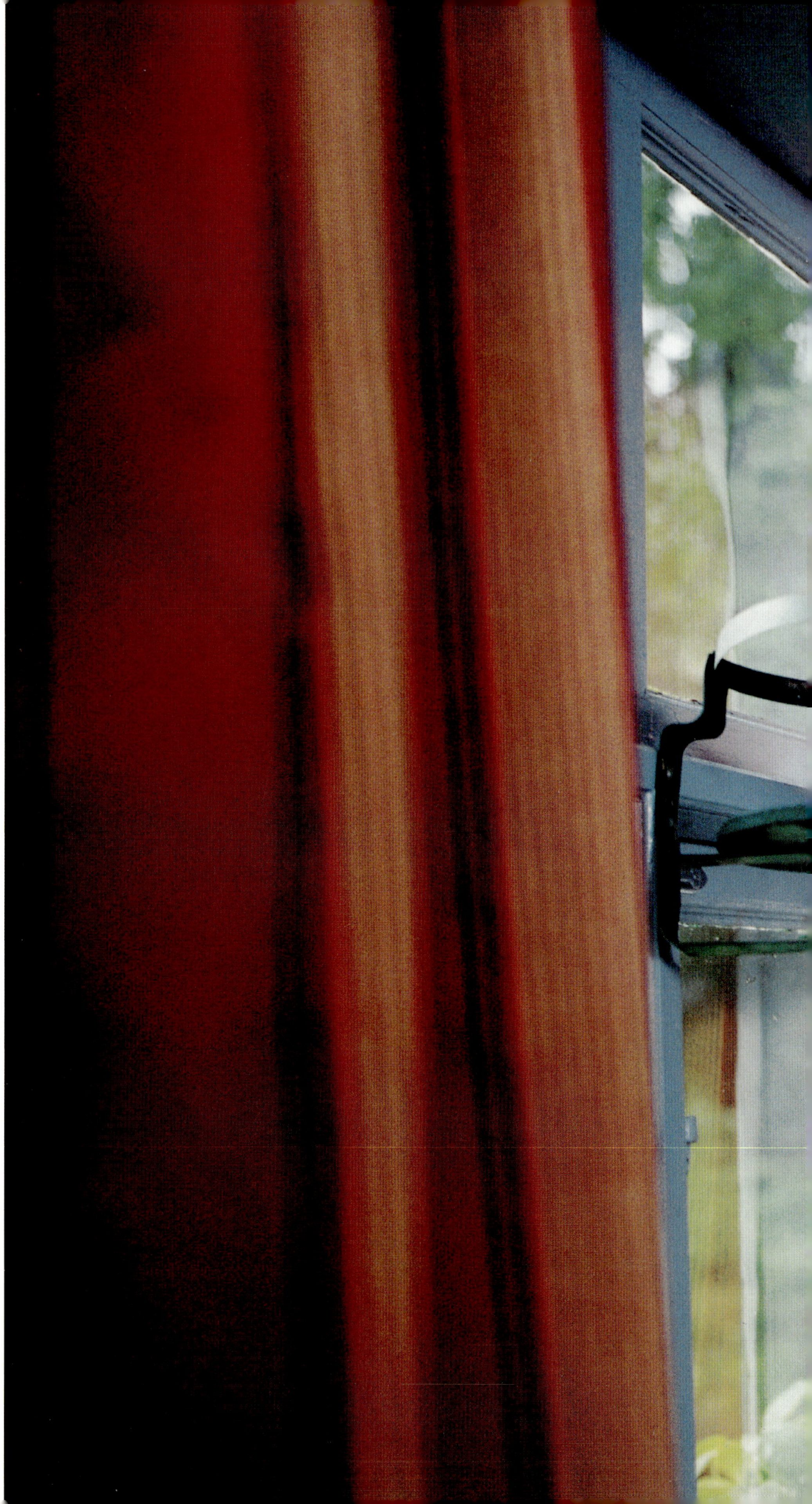

EIJA-LIISA AHTILA

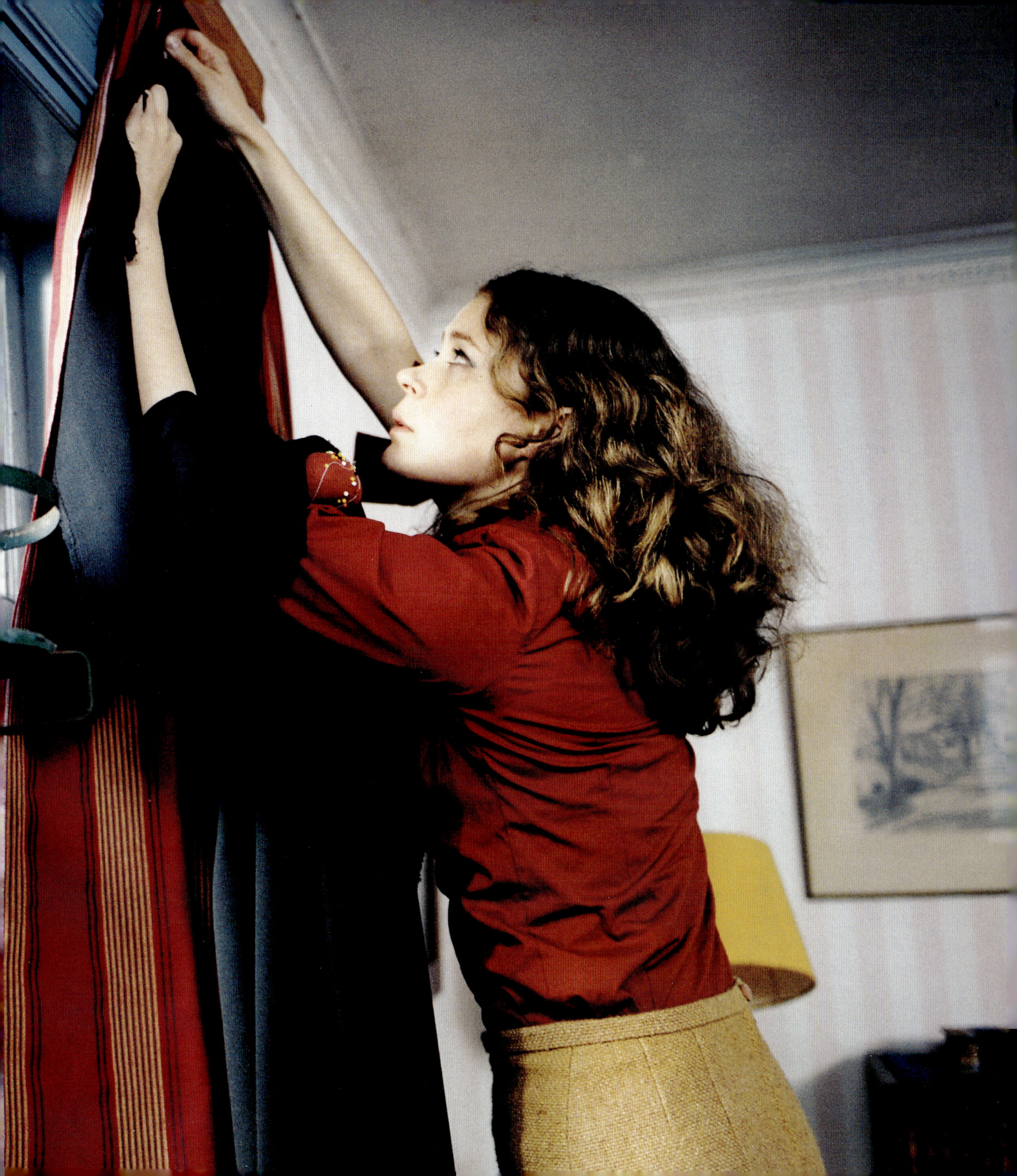

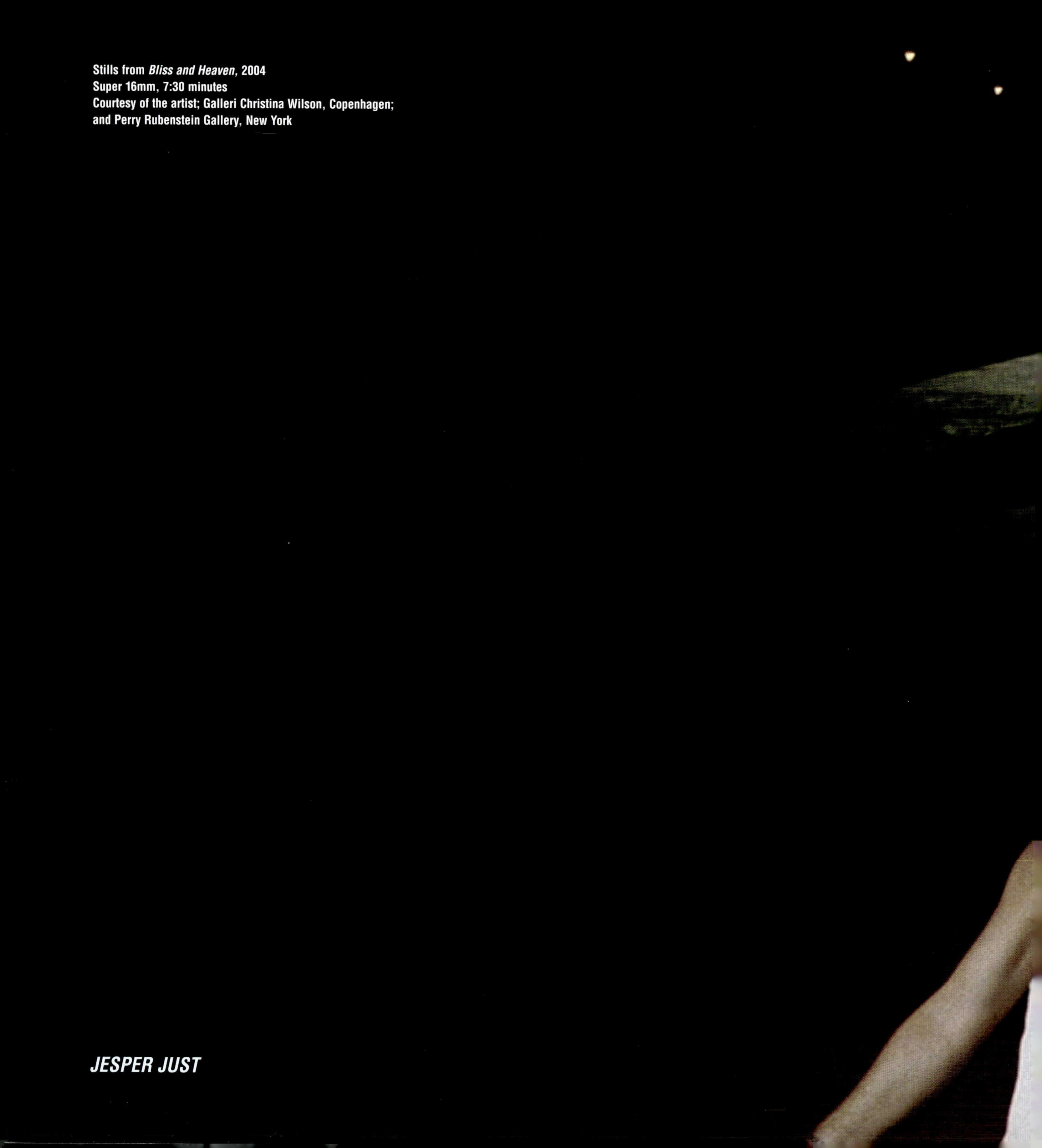

Stills from *Bliss and Heaven,* 2004
Super 16mm, 7:30 minutes
Courtesy of the artist; Galleri Christina Wilson, Copenhagen;
and Perry Rubenstein Gallery, New York

JESPER JUST

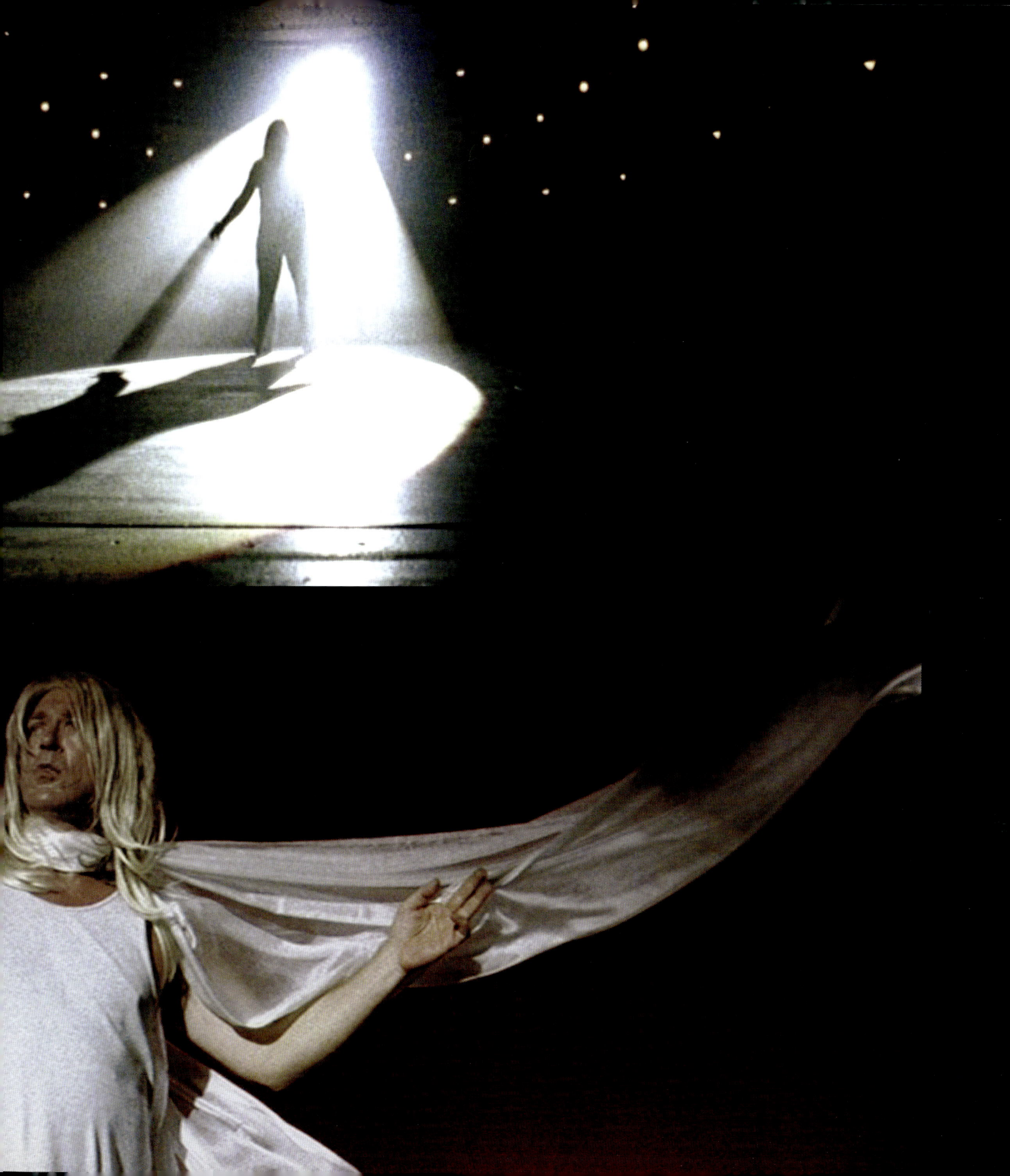

Stills from *No Man Is an Island II*, 2004
DVCAM, 4:00 minutes
Courtesy of the artist; Galleri Christina Wilson, Copenhagen; and Perry Rubenstein Gallery, New York

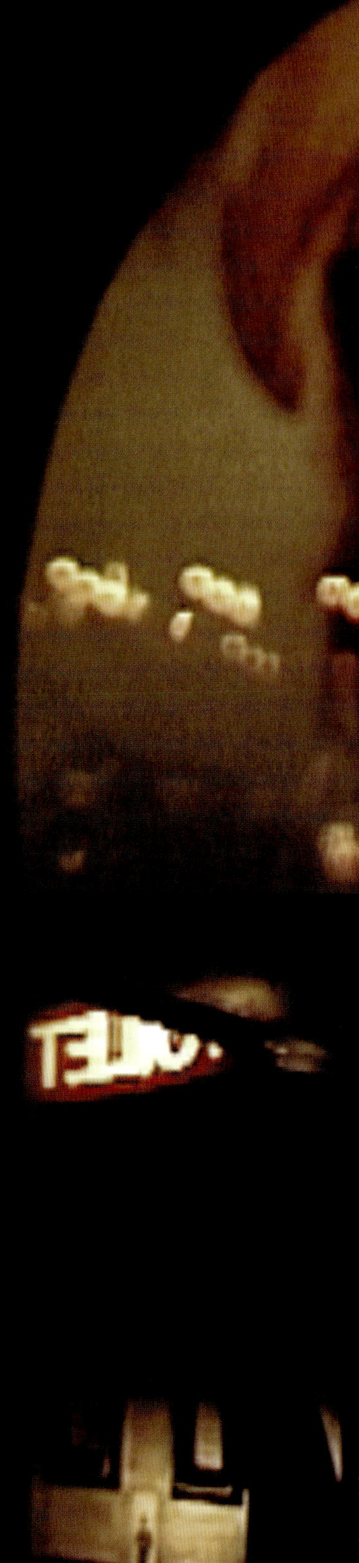

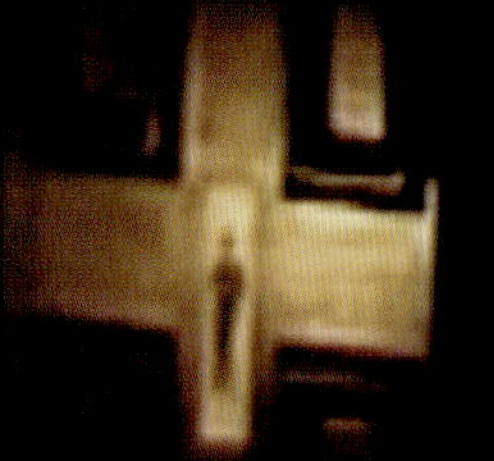

JESPER JUST

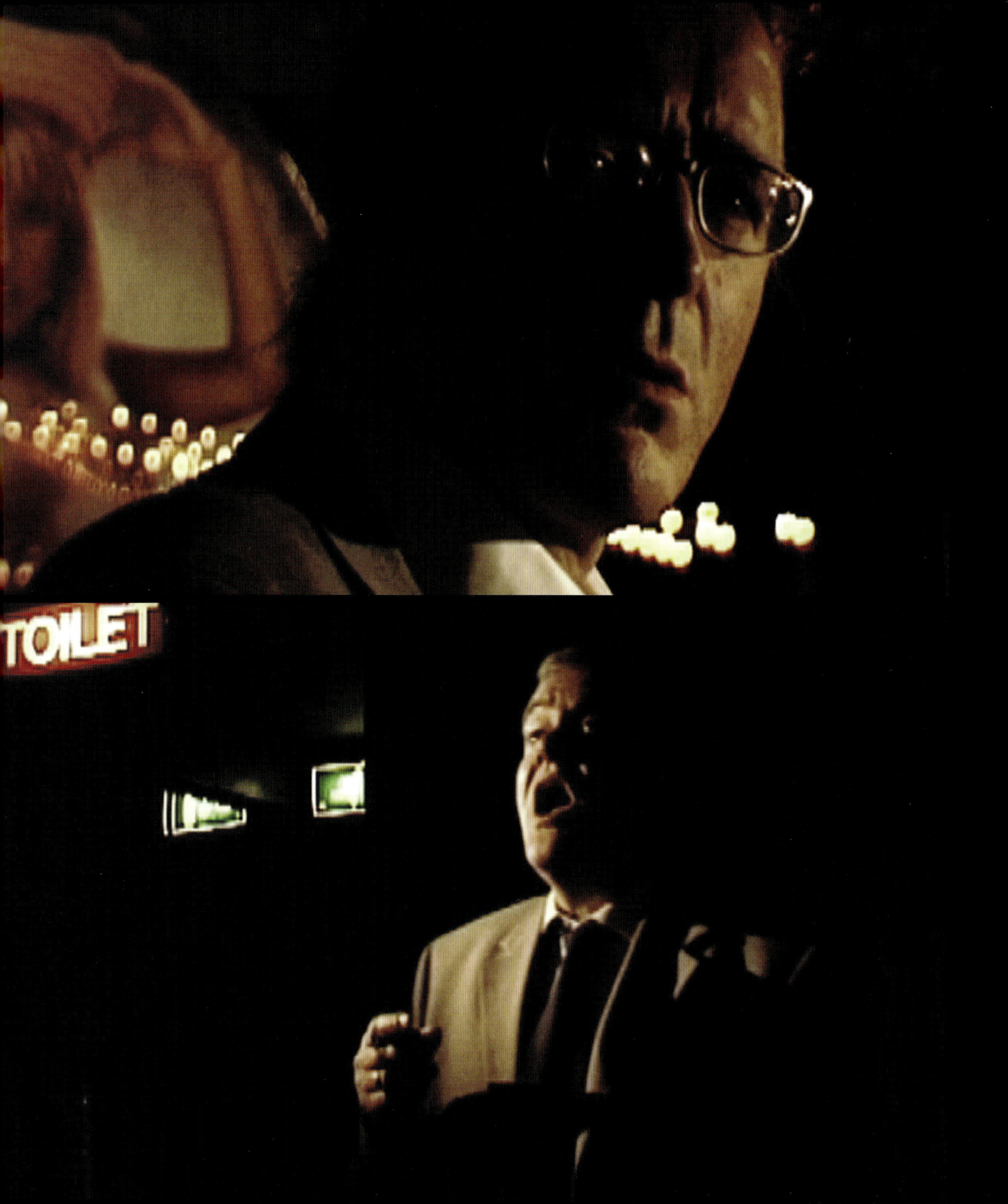
TOILET

Stills from *Something to Love*, 2005
Super 16mm, 8:10 minutes
Courtesy of the artist; Galleri Christina Wilson, Copenhagen; and Perry Rubenstein Gallery, New York

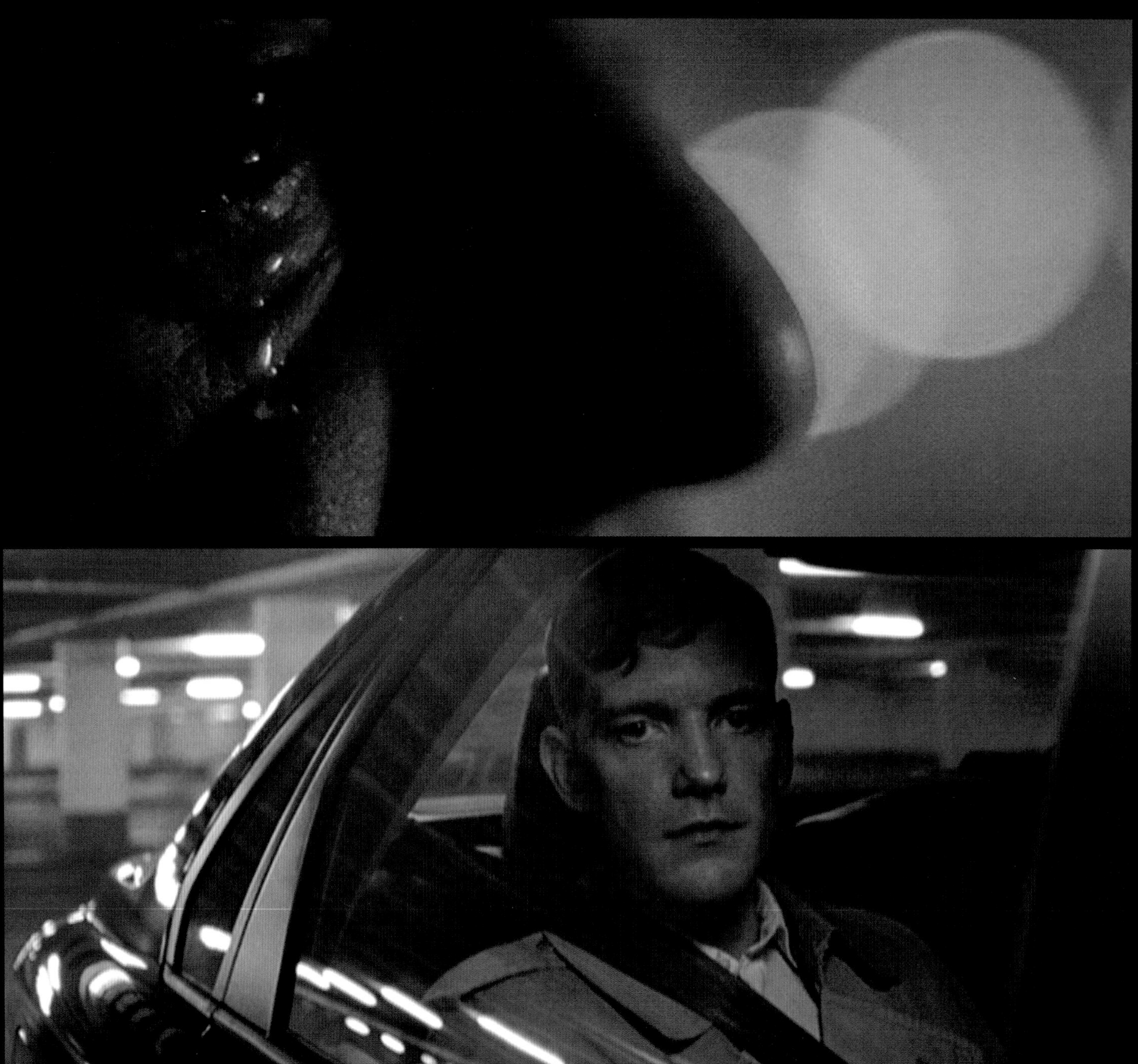

JESPER JUST

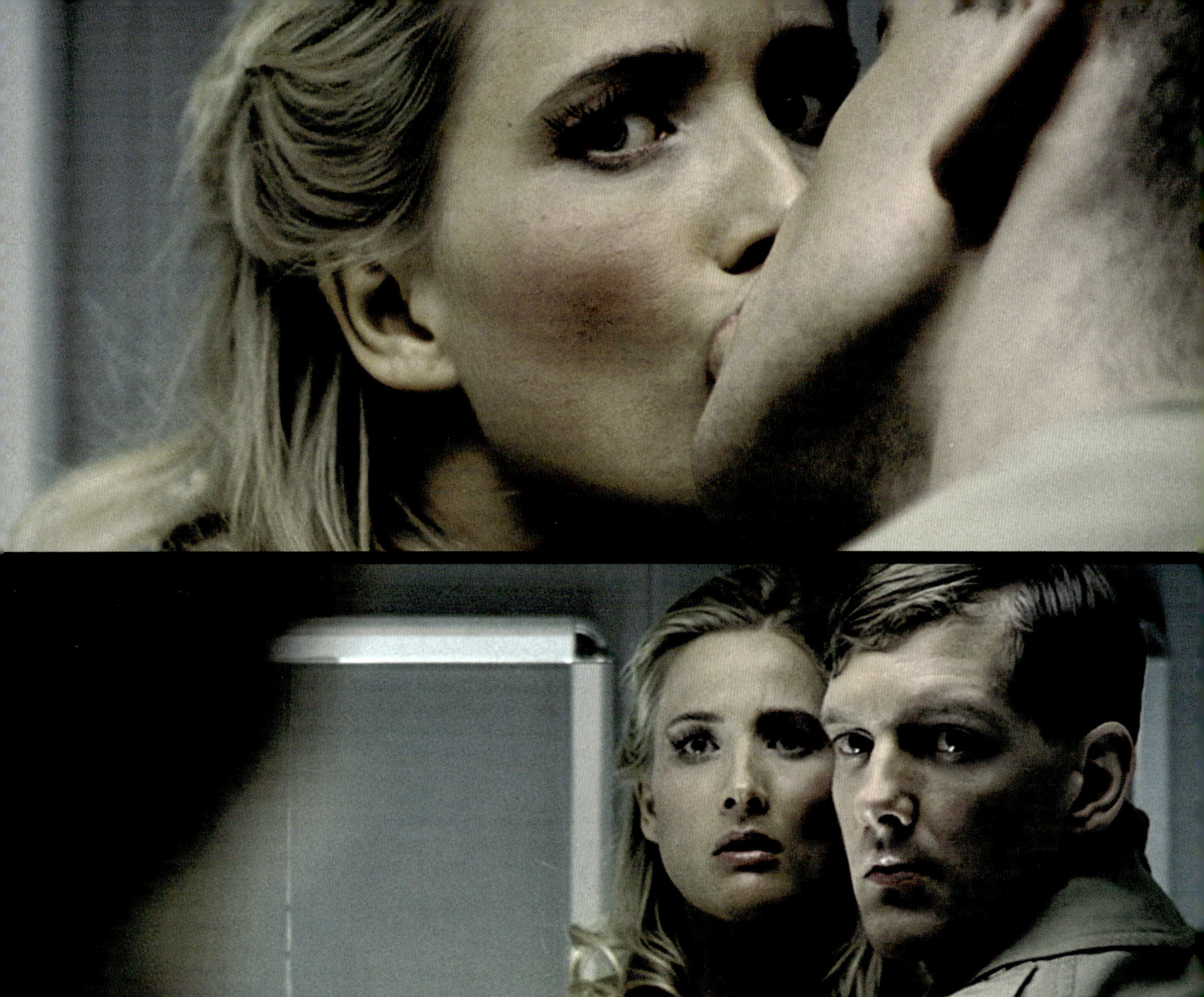

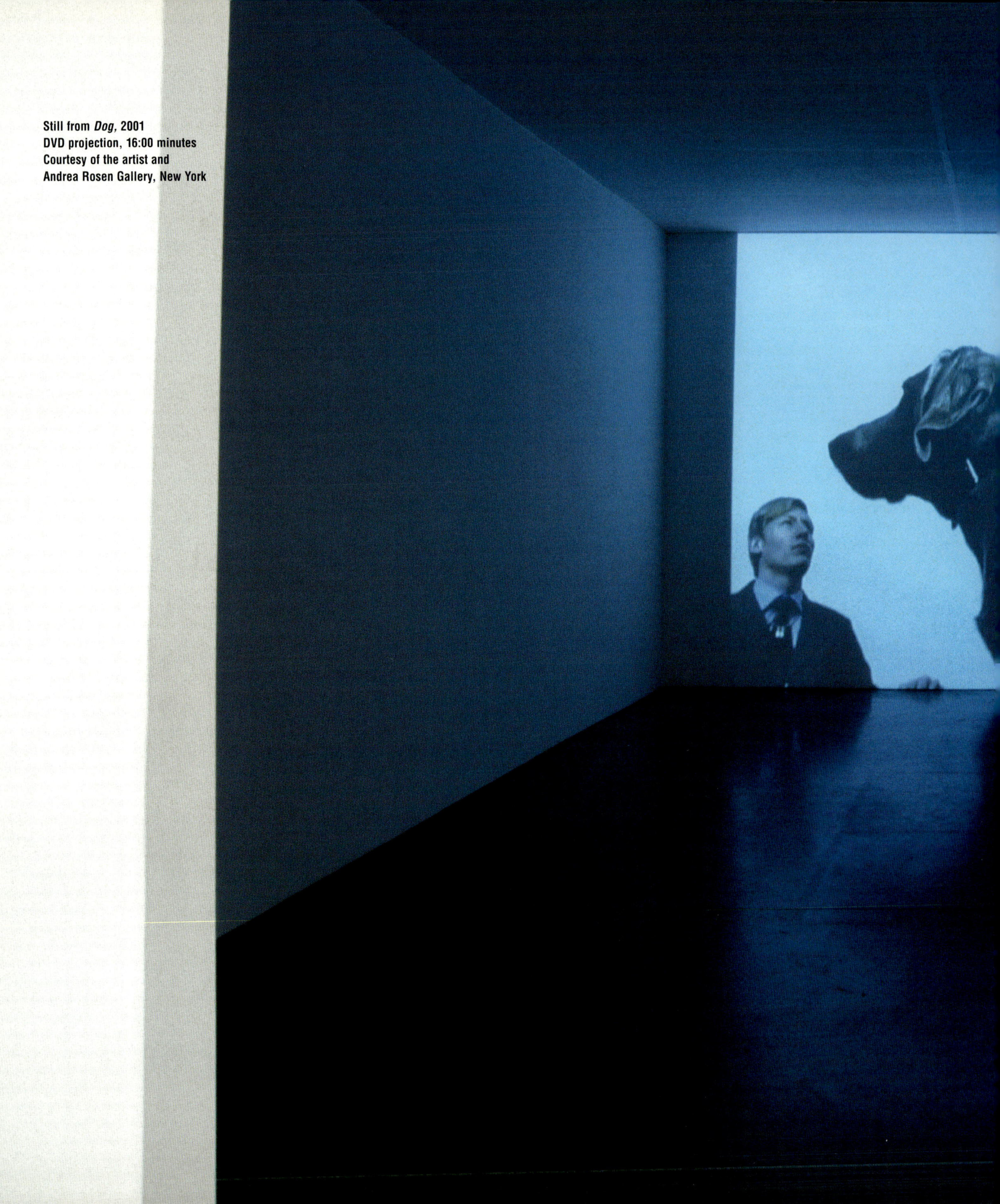

Still from *Dog,* 2001
DVD projection, 16:00 minutes
Courtesy of the artist and
Andrea Rosen Gallery, New York

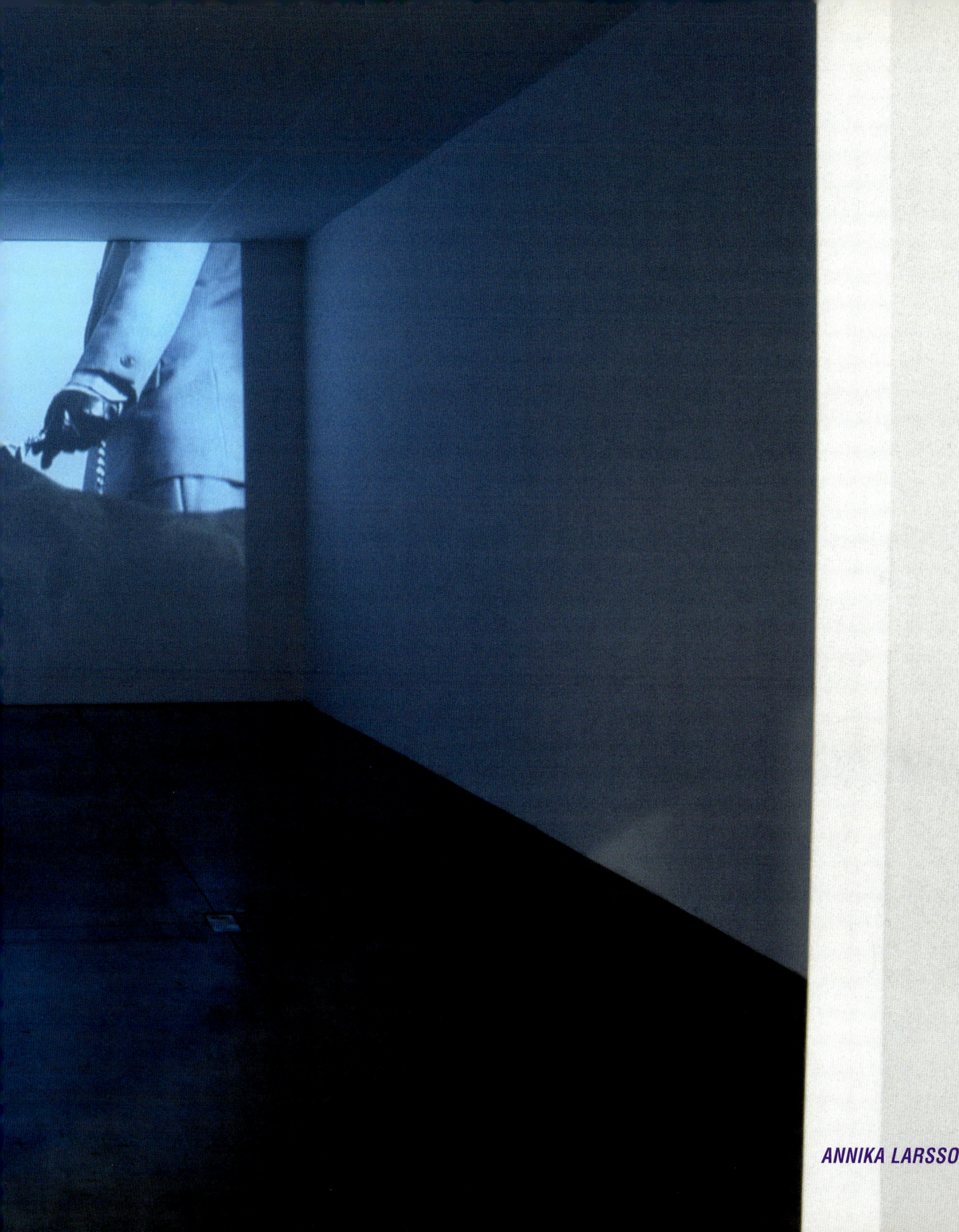

ANNIKA LARSSON

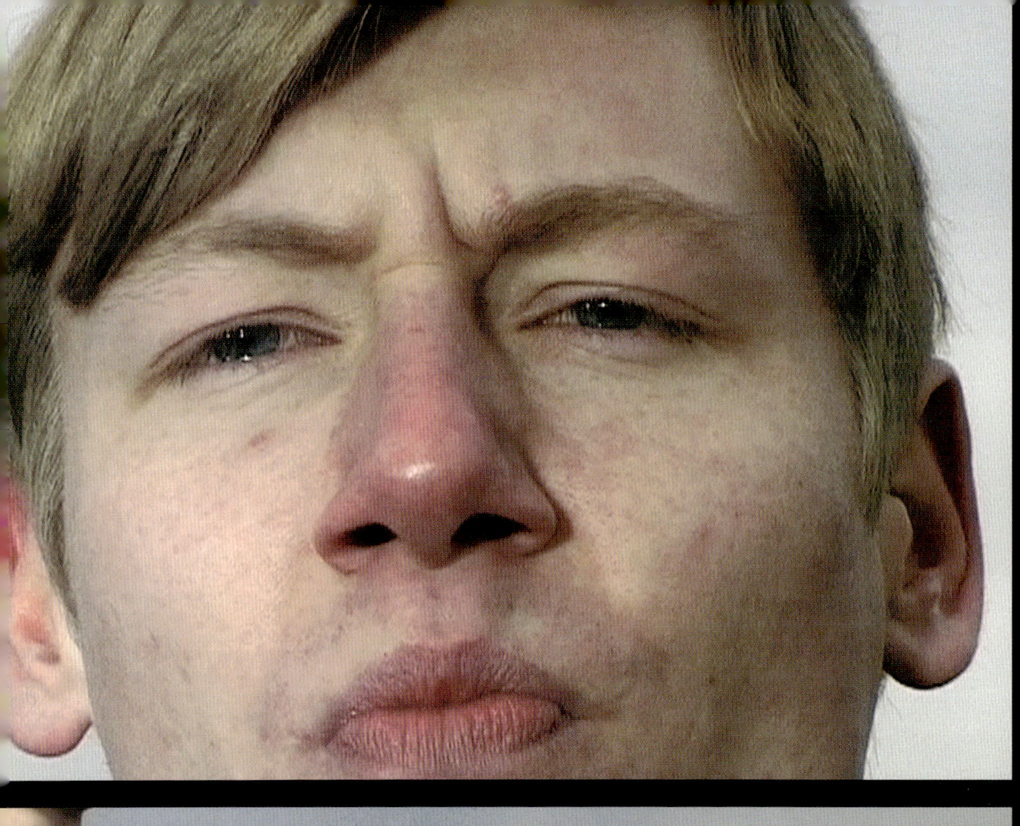
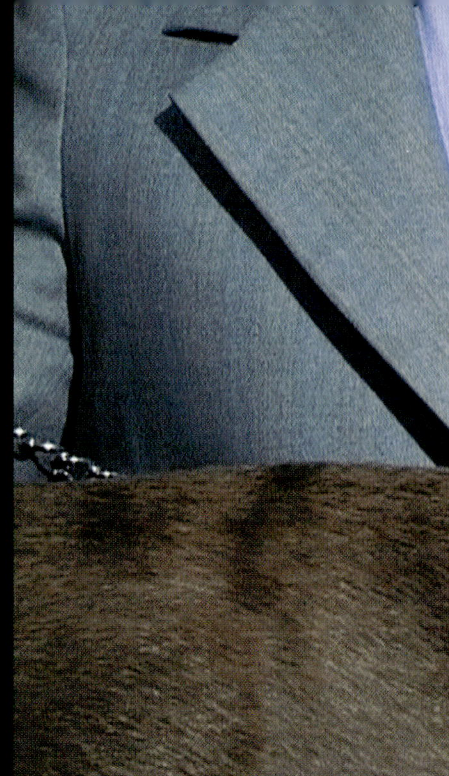
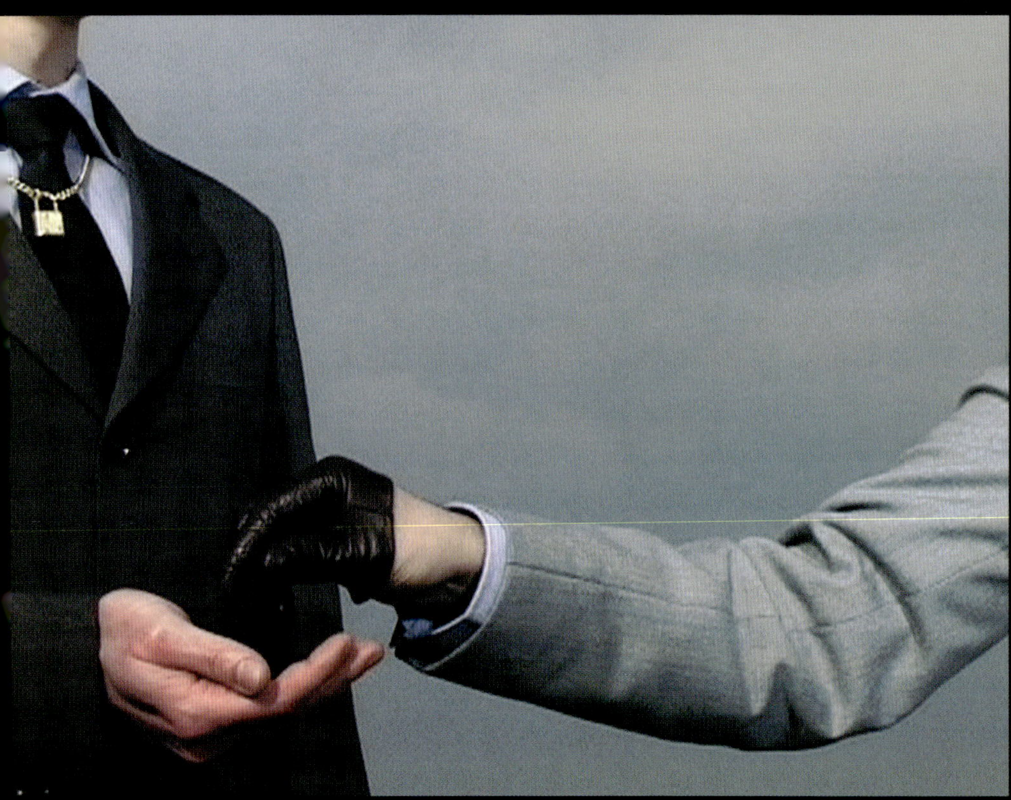
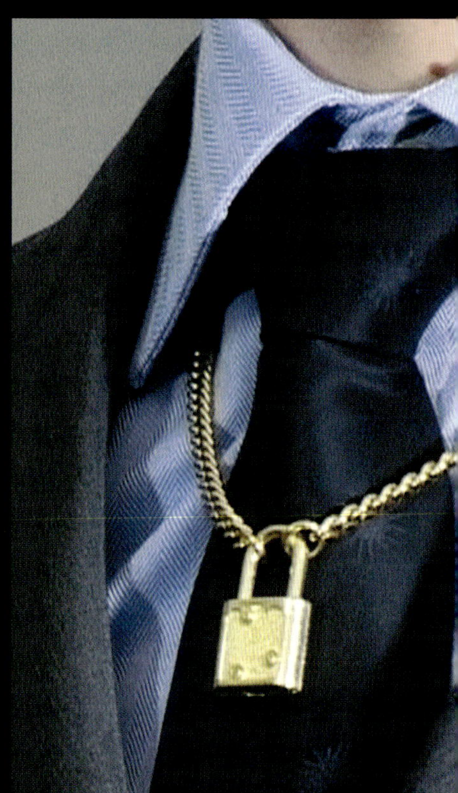

Stills from *Dog*, 2001; DVD projection, 16:00 minutes; courtesy of the artist and Andrea Rosen Gallery, New York

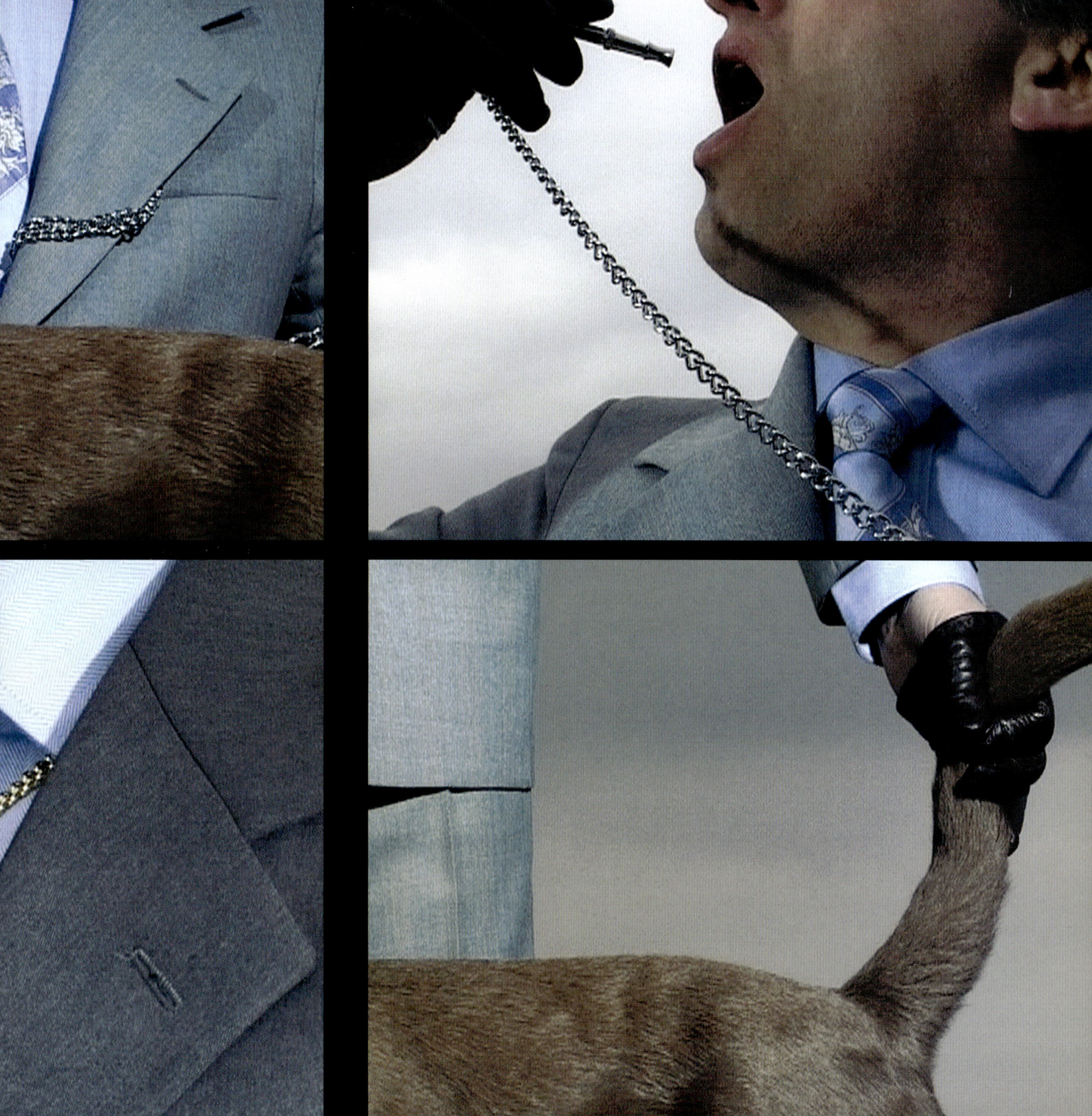

ANNIKA LARSSON

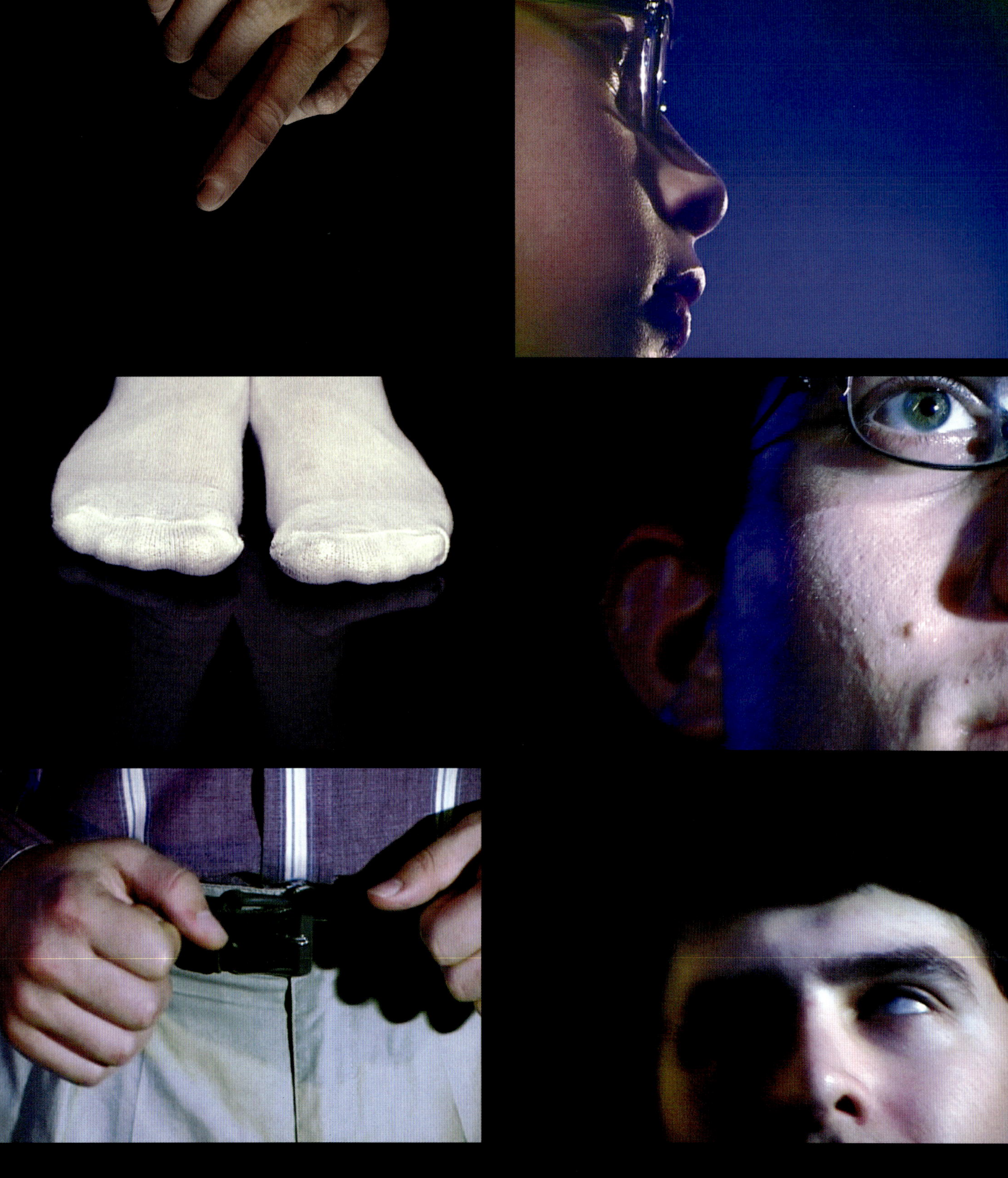

Stills from *New Gravity*, 2003; DVD loop, 29:30 minutes; courtesy of the artist and Andrea Rosen Gallery, New York

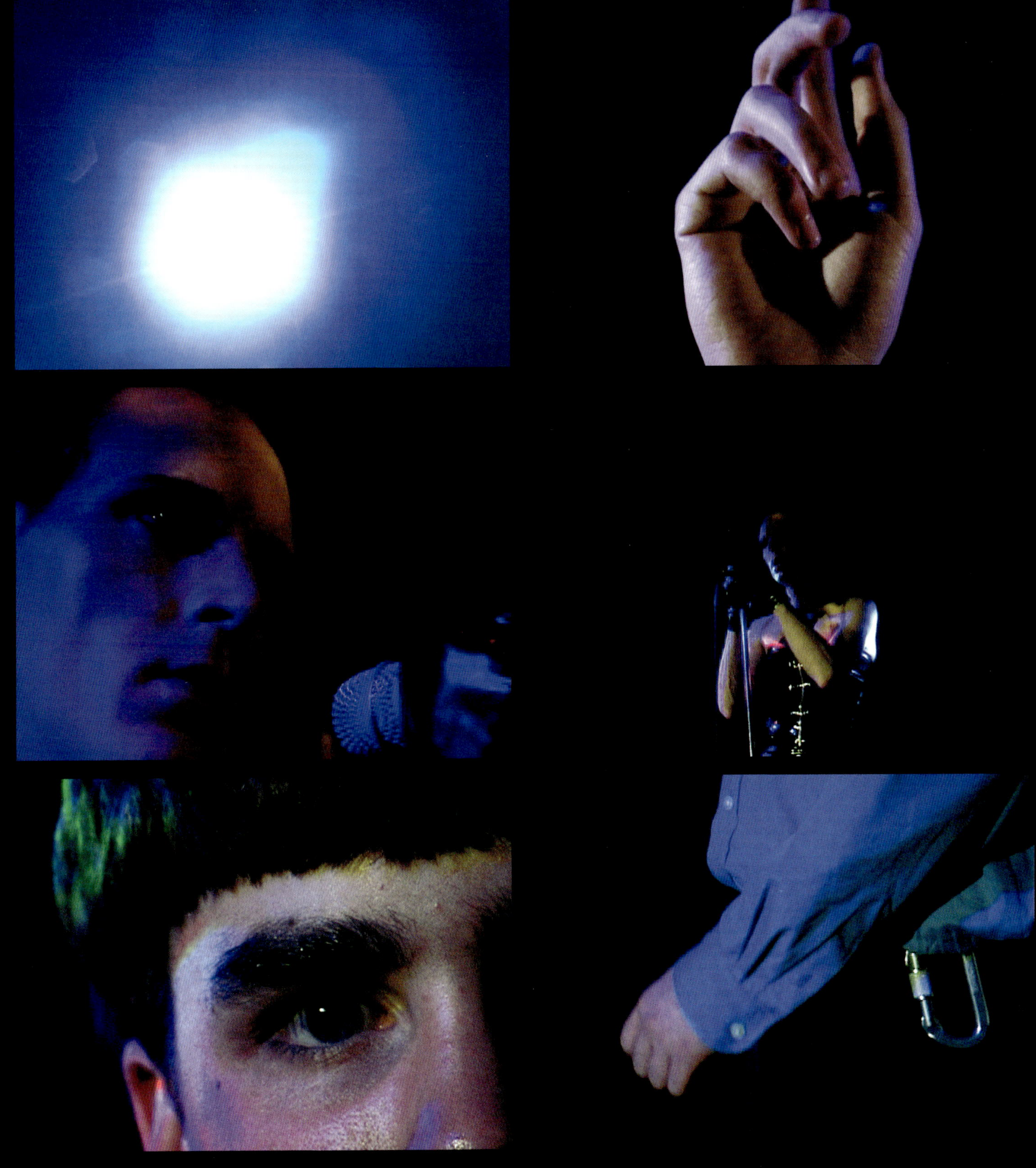

ANNIKA LARSSON

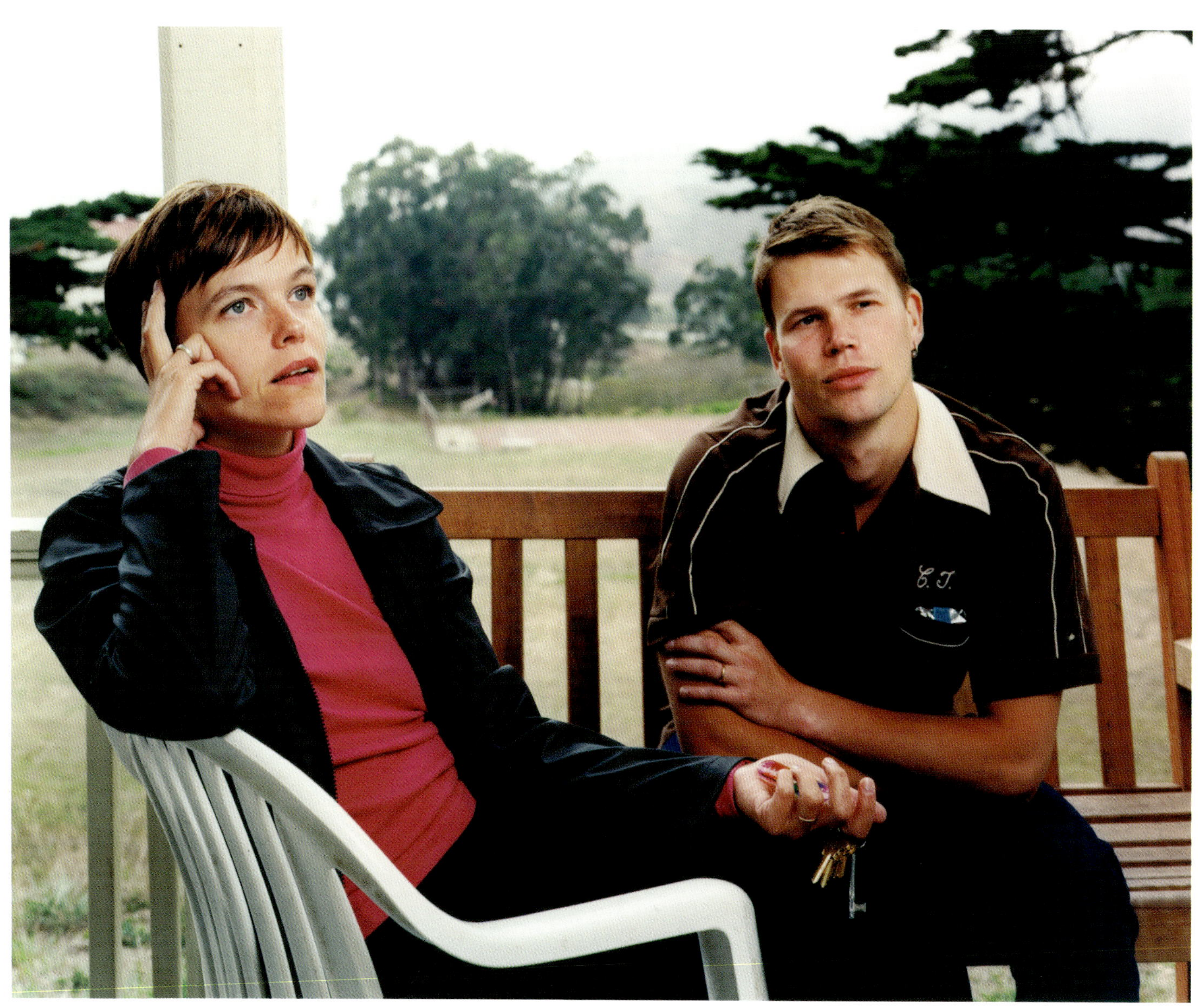

Portrait of Annika von Hausswolff and Johan Zetterquist from the series *Portraits in Nordic Light*, 1997
C print
46 x 56.5 in. (118 x 145 cm)
Courtesy of the artist

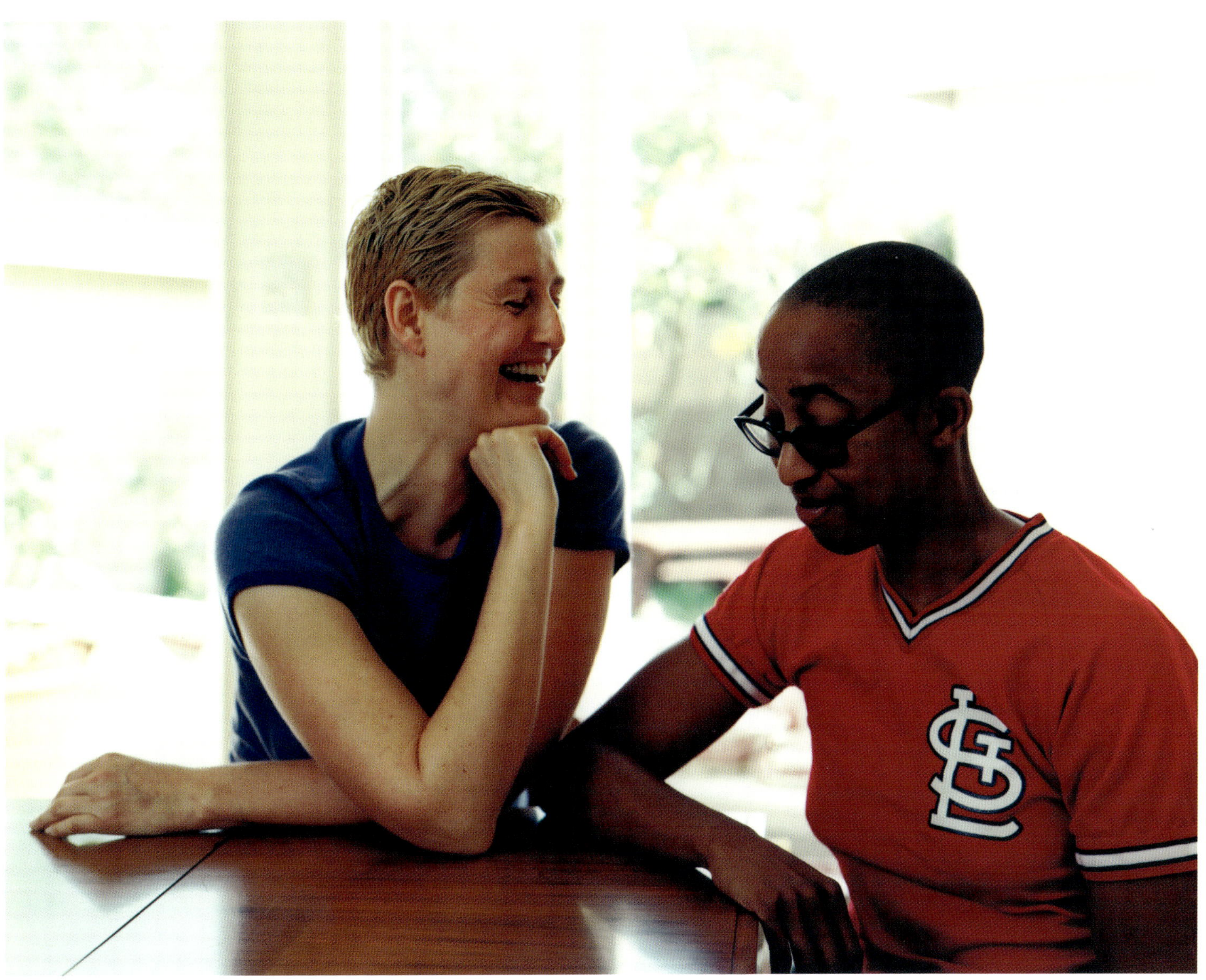

Double Portrait from the series *Portraits in Nordic Light*, 1998
C print
33.5 x 42.1 in. (86 x 108 cm)
Courtesy of the artist

ANNICA KARLSSON RIXON

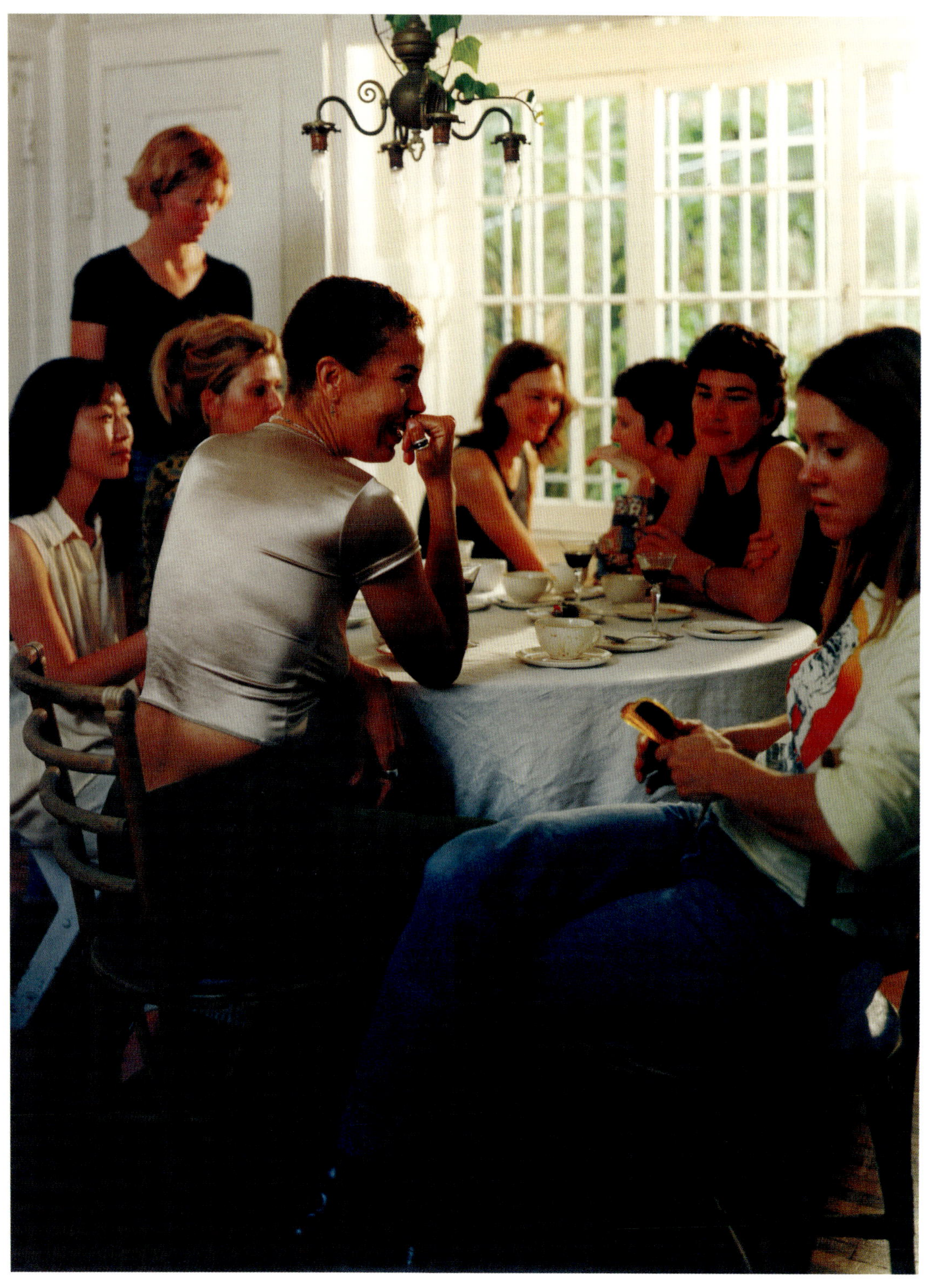

The Artists' Luncheon from the series *Portraits in Nordic Light*, 1997
C print
32 x 23.8 in. (82 x 61 cm)
Courtesy of the artist

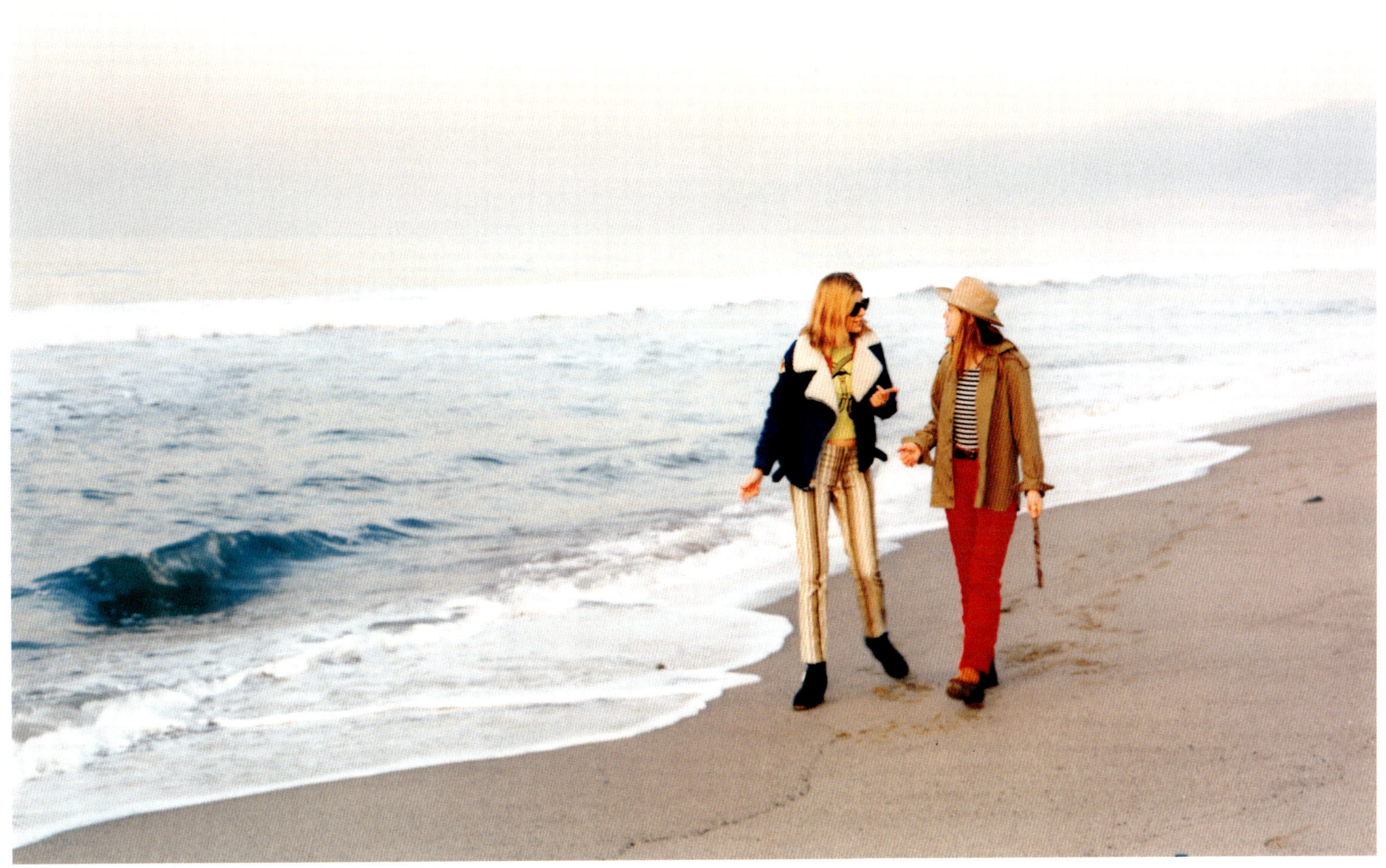

Winter Morning at Santa Monica Beach from the series *Portraits in Nordic Light*, 1997
C print
38.2 x 62.4 in. (98 x 160 cm)
Courtesy of the artist

ANNICA KARLSSON RIXON

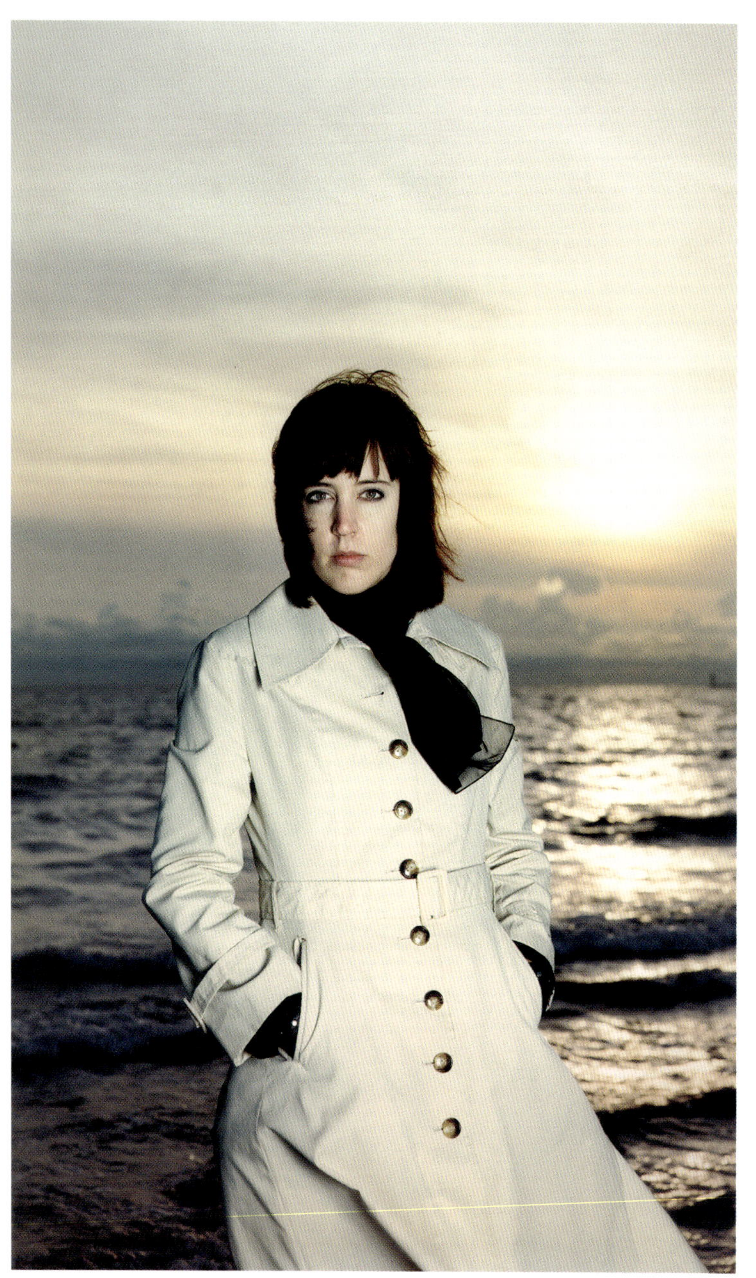

Annika Larsson by the Baltic Sea from the series *Annika by the Sea*, 2000
C print
78.75 x 47.25 in. (200 x 120 cm)
Courtesy of the artist

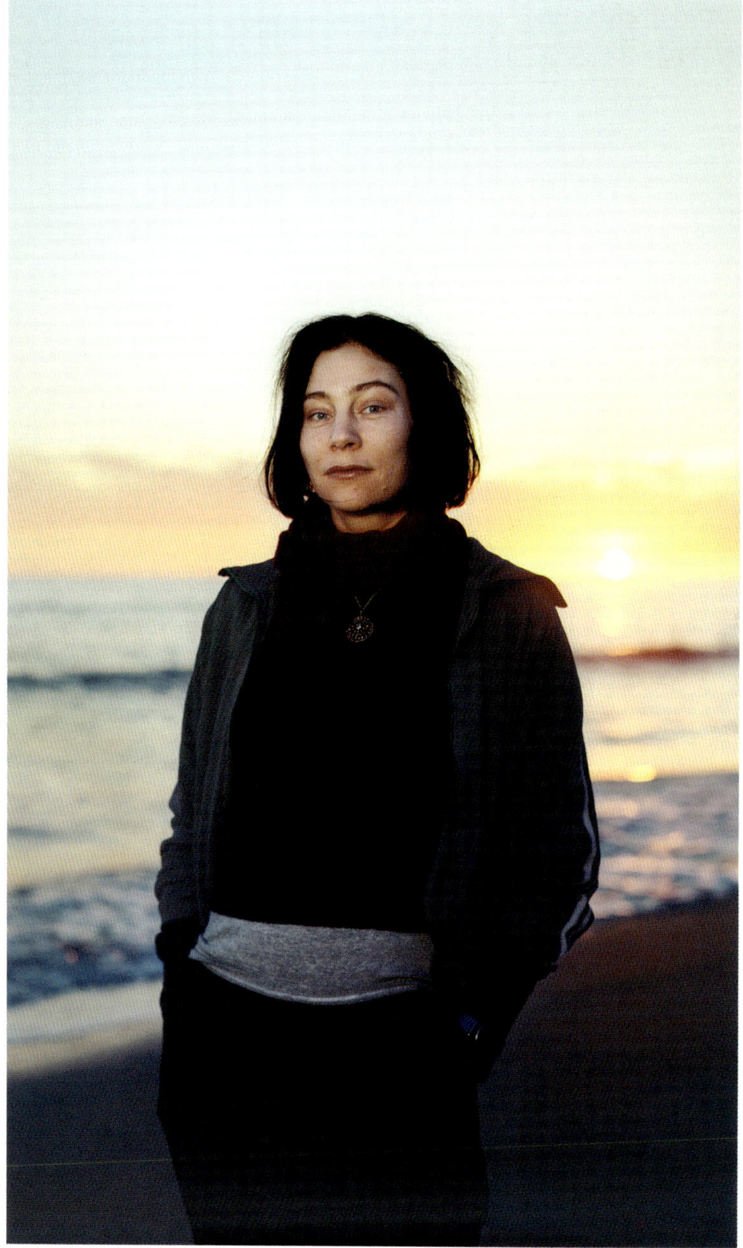

Annika Lundgren by the Pacific Ocean from the series *Annika by the Sea*, 1999
C print
78.75 x 47.25 in. (200 x 120 cm)
Courtesy of the artist

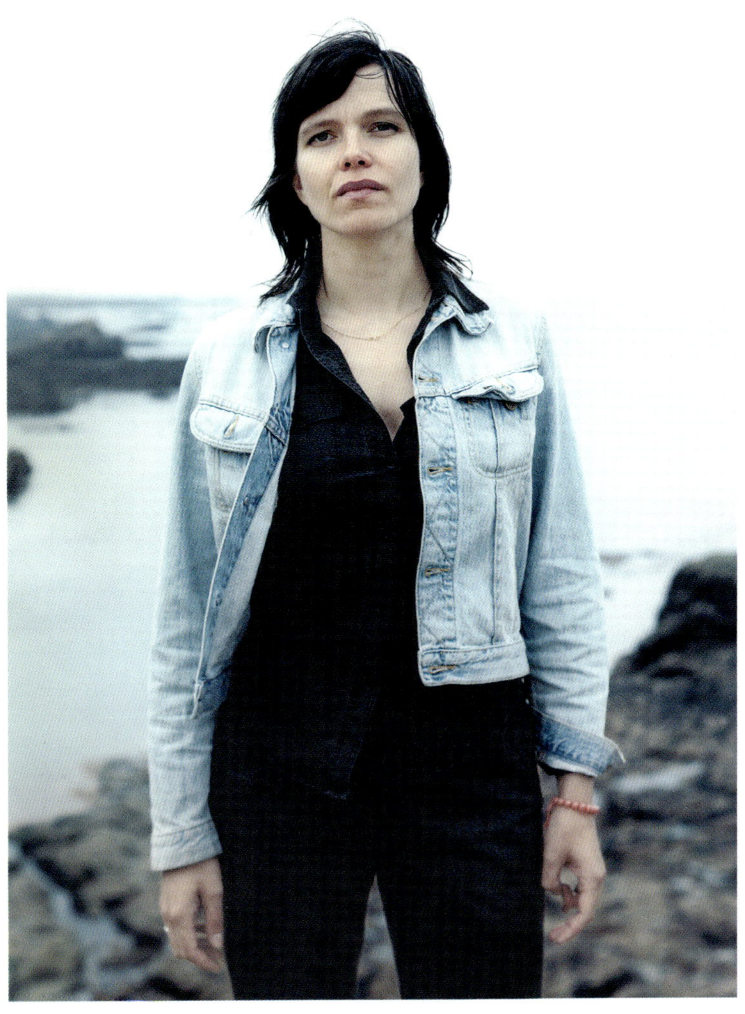

Annika von Hausswolff by the Atlantic Ocean from the series *Annika by the Sea*, 2000
C print
78.75 x 47.25 in. (200 x 120 cm)
Courtesy of the artist

ANNICA KARLSSON RIXON

CHECKLIST FOR THE EXHIBITION

EIJA-LIISA AHTILA
Lahja (The Present), 2001
Multimedia installation
Courtesy of the San Francisco Museum of Modern Art and Marian Goodman Gallery, New York

JESPER JUST
Bliss and Heaven, 2004
Super 16mm, 7:30 minutes
Courtesy of the artist; Galleri Christina Wilson, Copenhagen; and Perry Rubenstein Gallery, New York

No Man Is an Island II, 2004
DVCAM, 4:00 minutes
Courtesy of the artist; Galleri Christina Wilson, Copenhagen; and Perry Rubenstein Gallery, New York

Something to Love, 2005
Super 16mm, 8:10 minutes
Courtesy of the artist; Galleri Christina Wilson, Copenhagen; and Perry Rubenstein Gallery, New York

ANNIKA LARSSON
Dog, 2001
DVD projection, 16:00 minutes
Courtesy of the artist and Andrea Rosen Gallery, New York

New Gravity, 2003
DVD loop, 29:30 minutes
Courtesy of the artist and Andrea Rosen Gallery, New York

ANNICA KARLSSON RIXON
Annika Larsson by the Baltic Sea from the series *Annika by the Sea*, 2000
C print
78.75 x 47.25 in. (200 x 120 cm)
Courtesy of the artist

Double Portrait from the series *Portraits in Nordic Light*, 1998
C print
33.5 x 42.1 in. (86 x 108 cm)
Courtesy of the artist

Early Summer Evening in Los Angeles from the series *Portraits in Nordic Light*, 1997
C print
46.8 x 62.4 in. (120 x 160 cm)
Courtesy of the artist

Portrait of Annika von Hausswolff and Johan Zetterquist from the series *Portraits in Nordic Light*, 1997
C print
46 x 56.5 in. (118 x 145 cm)
Courtesy of the artist

The Artists' Luncheon from the series *Portraits in Nordic Light*, 1997
C print
32 x 23.8 in. (82 x 61 cm)
Courtesy of the artist

Winter Morning at Santa Monica Beach from the series *Portraits in Nordic Light*, 1997
C print
38.2 x 62.4 in. (98 x 160 cm)
Courtesy of the artist

ARTIST BIOGRAPHIES

EIJA-LIISA AHTILA was born in 1959 in Hameenlinna, Finland. She attended Helsinki University between 1980 and 1985 and then the London College of Printing, School of Management, Film and Video Department in London in 1990–91. In 1994–95 she participated in the American Film Institute's Advanced Technology Program in Los Angeles. The artist lives and works in Helsinki. Recent solo exhibitions have been held in London, Helsinki, Berlin, and Chicago. In addition, she participated in *Documenta 11* and the 48th Venice Biennale. She is represented by Marian Goodman Gallery, New York.

JESPER JUST was born in 1974 in Copenhagen and graduated from the Royal Danish Academy of Fine Arts in 2003. He lives and works in Copenhagen, and shows internationally. Recent solo exhibitions have taken place in Toronto; New York City; Torino, Italy; and Copenhagen. He is represented by Perry Rubenstein Gallery, New York, and Galleri Christina Wilson, Copenhagen.

ANNIKA LARSSON was born in 1972 in Stockholm and graduated from the Royal Academy of Fine Arts in Stockholm in 2000. She currently lives and works in New York. Her work has been featured all over the world, including solo exhibitions in Paris, London, Milan, Prague, and Copenhagen. She is represented by the Andrea Rosen Gallery in New York and Andréhn-Schiptjenko, Stockholm.

ANNICA KARLSSON RIXON earned an MFA in 1997 from the California Institute of the Arts in Valencia, California, and completed a BFA in 1998 at the Nordic School of Photography in Stockholm, Sweden. Her work has been exhibited in group shows throughout Sweden, as well as Paris, Oslo, New York, San Francisco, and Los Angeles. The artist lives and works in Gothenburg, Sweden, where she is a professor in the School of Photography at Gothenburg University.

Annica Karlsson Rixon, *The IASPIS Studio*, 2001
C print
39 x 46.8 in. (100 x 120 cm)
Courtesy of the artist

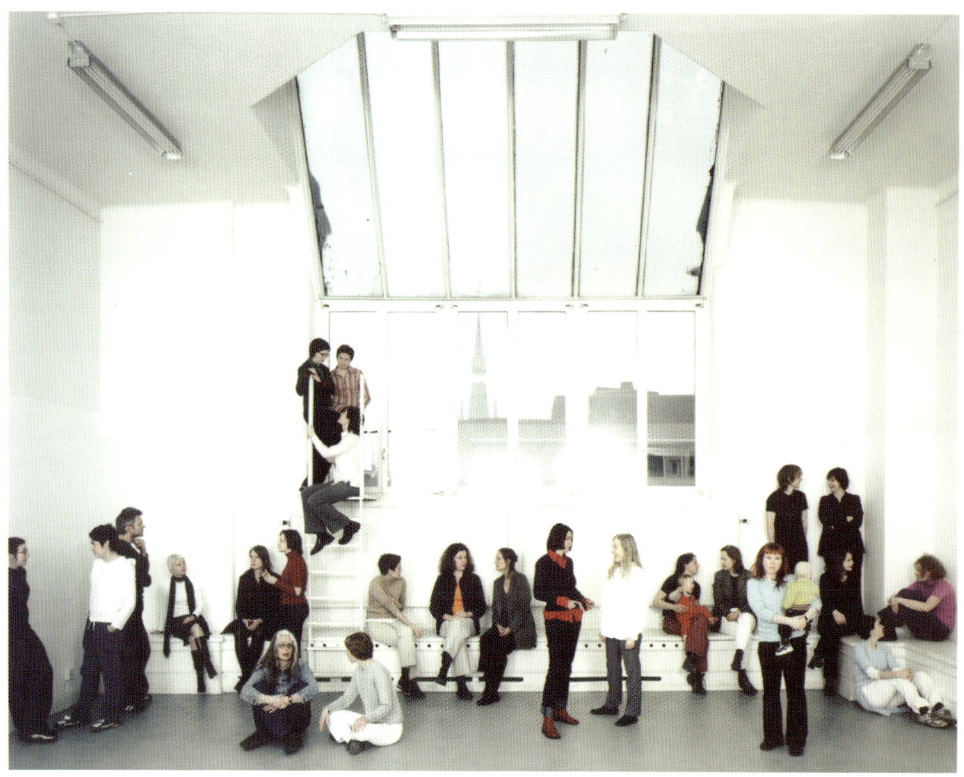

I would like to thank the many friends and colleagues who have encouraged and supported this project since its inception. Mark Johnson, Sharon Bliss, and the students in the Gallery Management class at San Francisco State University have worked tirelessly from the beginning to make the exhibition and catalogue possible. M.A. candidate Gina Basso assisted with library and Internet research. The title *Bent* first appeared as the title of the worldwide hit play that opened in London in 1979, and we use it here with a nod to that source. A special thanks goes to Eija-Liisa Ahtila, Jesper Just, Annika Larsson, and Annica Karlsson Rixon, who have given generously of their time and goodwill, and to collaborators on the catalogue Annika Öhrner and Linda Rugg. A special note of thanks also to Annika Öhrner for her assistance, coordination, and valuable feedback in Stockholm. A grant from the Scandinavian American Foundation in New York, and assistance from IASPIS in Stockholm, supported travel and research in Scandinavia. We are also grateful to the Moderna Museet in Stockholm for its support. Barbro Osher, the Swedish Consul in San Francisco, has been a generous patron and guiding light from the beginning. In Scandinavia, New York, and San Francisco, I have relied on the generosity, help, and advice of many people: Sara Arrhenius, Lena Johannesson, Yvonne Eriksson, Magdalena Malm, Martha Edelheit Nilsson, Janet Bishop and Neal Benezra at the San Francisco Museum of Modern Art, Sylvia Chivaratanond and the Perry Rubenstein Gallery, Laura Mackall and the Andrea Rosen Gallery, Tim Hawkinson at Klemens Gasser and Tanya Grunert, Inc., the Marian Goodman Gallery, and Crystal Eye in Helsinki.

— Whitney Chadwick